The French Revolution: A Very Short Introduction

VERY SHORT INTRODUCTIONS are for anyone wanting a stimulating and accessible way in to a new subject. They are written by experts, and have been published in more than 25 languages worldwide.

The series began in 1995, and now represents a wide variety of topics in history, philosophy, religion, science, and the humanities. Over the next few years it will grow to a library of around 200 volumes – a Very Short Introduction to everything from ancient Egypt and Indian philosophy to conceptual art and cosmology.

Very Short Introductions available now:

ANCIENT PHILOSOPHY
   Julia Annas
THE ANGLO-SAXON AGE
   John Blair
ANIMAL RIGHTS   David DeGrazia
ARCHAEOLOGY   Paul Bahn
ARCHITECTURE
   Andrew Ballantyne
ARISTOTLE   Jonathan Barnes
ART HISTORY   Dana Arnold
ART THEORY   Cynthia Freeland
THE HISTORY OF
   ASTRONOMY   Michael Hoskin
ATHEISM   Julian Baggini
AUGUSTINE   Henry Chadwick
BARTHES   Jonathan Culler
THE BIBLE   John Riches
BRITISH POLITICS
   Anthony Wright
BUDDHA   Michael Carrithers
BUDDHISM   Damien Keown
CAPITALISM   James Fulcher
THE CELTS   Barry Cunliffe
CHOICE THEORY
   Michael Allingham
CHRISTIAN ART   Beth Williamson
CLASSICS   Mary Beard and
   John Henderson
CLAUSEWITZ   Michael Howard
THE COLD WAR
   Robert McMahon

CONTINENTAL PHILOSOPHY
   Simon Critchley
COSMOLOGY   Peter Coles
CRYPTOGRAPHY
   Fred Piper and Sean Murphy
DADA AND SURREALISM
   David Hopkins
DARWIN   Jonathan Howard
DEMOCRACY   Bernard Crick
DESCARTES   Tom Sorell
DRUGS   Leslie Iversen
THE EARTH   Martin Redfern
EGYPTIAN MYTHOLOGY
   Geraldine Pinch
EIGHTEENTH-CENTURY
   BRITAIN   Paul Langford
THE ELEMENTS   Philip Ball
EMOTION   Dylan Evans
EMPIRE   Stephen Howe
ENGELS   Terrell Carver
ETHICS   Simon Blackburn
THE EUROPEAN UNION
   John Pinder
EVOLUTION
   Brian and Deborah Charlesworth
FASCISM   Kevin Passmore
THE FRENCH REVOLUTION
   William Doyle
FREUD   Anthony Storr
GALILEO   Stillman Drake
GANDHI   Bhikhu Parekh

Available soon:

AFRICAN HISTORY
  John Parker and Richard Rathbone
ANCIENT EGYPT   Ian Shaw
THE BRAIN   Michael O'Shea
BUDDHIST ETHICS
  Damien Keown
CHAOS   Leonard Smith
CHRISTIANITY   Linda Woodhead
CITIZENSHIP   Richard Bellamy
CLASSICAL ARCHITECTURE
  Robert Tavernor
CLONING   Arlene Judith Klotzko
CONTEMPORARY ART
  Julian Stallabrass
THE CRUSADES
  Christopher Tyerman
DERRIDA   Simon Glendinning
DESIGN   John Heskett
DINOSAURS   David Norman
DREAMING   J. Allan Hobson
ECONOMICS   Partha Dasgupta
THE END OF THE WORLD
  Bill McGuire
EXISTENTIALISM   Thomas Flynn
THE FIRST WORLD WAR
  Michael Howard
FREE WILL   Thomas Pink
FUNDAMENTALISM
  Malise Ruthven
HABERMAS   Gordon Finlayson

HIEROGLYPHS
  Penelope Wilson
HIROSHIMA   B. R. Tomlinson
HUMAN EVOLUTION
  Bernard Wood
INTERNATIONAL RELATIONS
  Paul Wilkinson
JAZZ   Brian Morton
MANDELA   Tom Lodge
MEDICAL ETHICS
  Tony Hope
THE MIND   Martin Davies
MYTH   Robert Segal
NATIONALISM   Steven Grosby
PERCEPTION   Richard Gregory
PHILOSOPHY OF RELIGION
  Jack Copeland and Diane Proudfoot
PHOTOGRAPHY
  Steve Edwards
THE RAJ   Denis Judd
THE RENAISSANCE
  Jerry Brotton
RENAISSANCE ART
  Geraldine Johnson
SARTRE   Christina Howells
THE SPANISH CIVIL WAR
  Helen Graham
TRAGEDY   Adrian Poole
THE TWENTIETH CENTURY
  Martin Conway

For more information visit our web site
www.oup.co.uk/vsi

William Doyle

# THE FRENCH
# REVOLUTION

## A Very Short Introduction

# OXFORD
UNIVERSITY PRESS

Great Clarendon Street, Oxford OX2 6DP

Oxford University Press is a department of the University of Oxford.
It furthers the University's objective of excellence in research, scholarship,
and education by publishing worldwide in

Oxford New York

Auckland Bangkok Buenos Aires Cape Town Chennai
Dar es Salaam Delhi Hong Kong Istanbul Karachi Kolkata
Kuala Lumpur Madrid Melbourne Mexico City Mumbai Nairobi
São Paulo Shanghai Taipei Tokyo Toronto

Oxford is a registered trade mark of Oxford University Press
in the UK and in certain other countries

Published in the United States
by Oxford University Press Inc., New York

British Library Cataloguing in Publication Data
Data available

Library of Congress Cataloging in Publication Data
Data available

ISBN 978-0-19-285396-7

15 17 19 20 18 16 14

Typeset by RefineCatch Ltd, Bungay, Suffolk
Printed in Great Britain by
Ashford Colour Press Ltd, Gosport, Hampshire

# Preface

To produce a very short book about a subject on which one has
written at varying lengths before is more of a challenge than it might
seem. We can all think of people who have 'written the same book'
several times over in different forms; and we all dread becoming like
them. So I have not set out primarily to retell a familiar story, although
anything calling itself an introduction must to some extent do that.
My concern has been much more to discuss why the French Revolution
mattered, and has continued to matter in innumerable ways in the
two centuries since it occurred. The whole story of the Revolution,
both as a series of late eighteenth-century events and as a set of ideas,
images, and memories in the minds of posterity, is a powerful
argument for the importance of history, as well as a striking example
of its complexity. Whether it will remain as relevant for understanding
the twenty-first century as it was for the nineteenth and twentieth
is perhaps, as a Chinese sage is reputed to have observed, too early
to say.

The first time I studied the French Revolution seriously was in my final
year as an undergraduate. It was lit up by the providential appearance
of Norman Hampson's *Social History of the French Revolution*. I am not
surprised that it is still in print as its author enters his eightieth year.
Later it was my privilege to be Norman's colleague at York. In
gratitude for that, and the years of friendship since, I dedicate this

book to him. I hope he will not find association with a work slighter than any of his own the least welcome of what are sure to be many birthday presents.

William Doyle, Bath, 8 April 2001

# Contents

# List of illustrations

1. Louis XVI: The absolute monarch in all his glory.

# Chapter 1
## Echoes

'Mr Worthing,' says Lady Bracknell in *The Importance of Being Earnest* (1895), 'I feel somewhat bewildered by what you have just told me. To be born, or at any rate bred, in a handbag, whether it had handles or not, seems to me to display a contempt for the ordinary decencies of life that reminds one of the worst excesses of the French Revolution. And I presume you know what that unfortunate movement led to?'

Presumably Mr Worthing did. Every person of good general knowledge in the nineteenth century knew something about the great upheaval which had marked the last years of the eighteenth. Serious Victorians would have felt it a duty to instruct themselves about what had happened in France, and why, in and after 1789; and how the ensuing turmoil had been brought to an end only by the generation-long 'Great War' against Napoleon which had marked the lives of their parents or grandparents. Mr Worthing, nibbling his cucumber sandwiches and dreaming of marrying Lady Bracknell's daughter, would not have been so curious. But probably even he would have had some idea of what the worst excesses of the French Revolution had been, and of how they had affronted life's ordinary decencies. He would have known that there had been a popular uprising leading to mob rule, the overthrow of monarchy and persecution of the nobility. He would have known that the chosen instrument of revolutionary vengeance was the guillotine, that relentless mechanical decapitator which made the streets of Paris run with royal and aristocratic blood. The creator of Mr Ernest Worthing and Lady Bracknell (her ancestors, had they been French, could scarcely have hoped to avoid the dread instrument . . . ) ended his days in morose exile in Paris. There, Oscar Wilde was surrounded by symbols and images deliberately designed by the rulers of the Third Republic to evoke the memory of the First, the Revolution's creation. The coinage and public buildings were emblazoned with the slogan *Liberty, Equality, Fraternity*. On festive occasions the streets fluttered with red, white, and blue bunting, the colours of the tricolour flag adopted by the French Nation in 1789. On 14th July each year a national festival celebrated the fall on that day in 1789 of the Bastille, a forbidding state prison stormed and then levelled by the people in the name of liberty. At such moments of public jubilation French patriots sang the *Marseillaise*, the battle hymn of a war against tyranny launched in 1792. And undoubtedly the greatest sight in Paris when Wilde lived there was the world's tallest building, the Eiffel Tower, the centrepiece of a great exhibition which had marked the Revolution's first centenary in 1889.

Nobody who lived in France, or visited it, could avoid these echoes; or echoes of Napoleon, who had marched under the tricolour, had tamed and harnessed the energies unleashed by the Revolution, and whose nephew Napoleon III had ruled for 22 years before the Third Republic was established. Nobody who knew anything of France even at second hand (if only through learning what was still the first foreign language of choice throughout most of the world) could fail to imbibe some sense that this country had been marked by a traumatic convulsion only just beyond living memory. Many believed, or felt, that this must have been for the best and somehow necessary. Everybody knew and was shocked by the story of how Queen Marie-Antoinette, guillotined amid popular jubilation in 1793, had said 'Let them eat cake' when told that the people had no bread. (Everybody knows it still, and nobody cares that it was an old story even before she was born, heard by Jean-Jacques Rousseau as early as 1740.) New nations have been proud to proclaim their emancipation, or to anticipate it like the patriots of Brussels in

1789, or Milan in 1796, by adopting tricolour flags. This banner of liberty still flies from Rome to Mexico City, from Bucharest to Dublin. Poles, who first sang the *Marseillaise* in 1794 as they resisted the carve-up of their country, sang it again in 1956 in revolt against Soviet tyranny. In 1989, as France commemorated the Revolution's 200th anniversary, the same anthem of defiance was heard in Beijing, among the doomed student protesters in Tiananmen Square. Few countries have failed to experience some sort of revolution since 1789, and in all of them there have been people looking back to what happened in France then and subsequently for inspiration, models, patterns, or warnings.

## Cross-Channel perspectives

Most detached from all this have been the world's English-speaking countries. Their last revolutions, except in Ireland, took place before 1789, and even English-speaking contemporaries who sympathized with the French saw them as catching up with liberties proclaimed in England in 1688, or America in 1776. In any case such sympathizers were always in a minority. The mould for most English-speaking attitudes was cast as early as 1790, some years before the Revolution's 'worst excesses', by Edmund Burke's *Reflections on the Revolution in France*. Outraged at the claims of reformers that the French were merely carrying on the work of the 'Glorious' British revolution of 1688 and the American rebels whose cause he had supported in the 1770s, Burke asserted that the French Revolution was something entirely new and different. Earlier revolutions in the anglophone world had sought to preserve a heritage of liberty from attack. By the new French standards, indeed, they had not been revolutions at all; for the French were seeking to establish what they called liberty by wholesale destruction. With caution, and respect for the wisdom of their ancestors, they might have corrected the few and venial faults of their former institutions, and come to run their affairs as freely and peaceably as the British ran theirs. But they had chosen to follow the untried dreams of rationalizing, self-styled 'philosophers' who had sapped faith in monarchy, the social order, and God Himself.

The result had been anarchy and the envious rule of the 'swinish multitude'. Burke predicted worse to come, and foretold that it would take a military dictatorship to end it all. Even he did not foresee how bloody matters would become, but he was right about the eventual triumph of a general. Burke came, therefore, to be revered as a prophet as well as a critic; even if the superiority of the British over the French way of doing things seemed only to be fully vindicated 18 years after his death, on the field of Waterloo.

But the French were incorrigible, and in 1830 the tricolour was unfurled again over a new, though briefer, Parisian revolution. Why had it come back to haunt the future? As the generation that had made or experienced the original cataclysm died away, historians began to appropriate it for analysis. Most of them are now forgotten, and the one who is not commands little respect among later practitioners of his craft. But Thomas Carlyle did more than anyone else to fix the popular idea of what the French Revolution was like. In his wild, inimitable style, *The French Revolution. A History* (1837) painted a vision of mindless and vengeful chaos. He did not follow Burke in trying to defend the ancien régime, the order that the revolutionaries destroyed. He thought it was rotten, and deserved its fate. While courtiers minced, and windbags prated, the hungry masses brooded on their oppression: 'unspeakable confusion is everywhere weltering within, and through so many cracks in the surface sulphur-smoke is issuing.' The Revolution was an explosion of popular violence, understandable if scarcely defensible resentment. Those who attempted to lead or guide it were mostly simpletons or scoundrels, all to be pitied for their presumption. The most frightful figure of all was Robespierre, who tried to rule through terror, and who was now fixed forever in non-French minds as the 'sea-green incorruptible' (in reference to his complexion as well as to his power). He sent his victims to their fate, and finally followed them there himself in tumbrils (a half-forgotten word for a tipping cart, never afterwards used except in this context). 'Red Nightcaps howl dire approval' as the tumbrils pass: this means sansculottes, men who did

4

2. Cross-Channel contrasts as seen from London by the caricaturist James Gillray in the 1790s.

not wear aristocratic kneebreeches but flaunted their patriotism with red caps of liberty. They and their screaming womenfolk were driven on by visceral lust for social revenge. Carlyle only recognized three men as capable of directing these forces of nature. One was Mirabeau, whose death in 1791 left his promise unfulfilled. Another was Danton, who saved France with his energy from foreign invasion in 1792, but was engulfed two years later by the terror: 'with all his dross he was a Man; fiery-real, from the great fire-bosom of Nature herself.' (At the time of Carlyle's writing, Georg Büchner was presenting German speakers with *Dantons Tod* [*Danton's Death*, 1835], a play in which Danton is depicted as too heroic a figure for the petty beings like Robespierre who combined to kill him.) Finally there was Napoleon, who brought the army into politics in 1795, ending the last Parisian insurrection with a 'whiff of grapeshot'.

## Dramatic depictions

The idiosyncratic vigour of Carlyle's writing leaves an impression of years of ceaseless turmoil, with blood and violence, merciless 'sansculottism', and baying mobs a daily sight. It was irresistibly dramatic. But Carlyle also had an eye for the pathos of innocent victims falling prey to forces men could not control. Even Robespierre receives a twinge of sympathy as he rumbles towards the guillotine in his new, sky-blue coat. The book thrilled and appalled its readers, and it sold, as well as read, like a novel. Novelists themselves admired it, and none more so than Charles Dickens.

Dickens' *A Tale of Two Cities* (1859), in fact, offered by far the most influential image that posterity has of the French Revolution. From Burke it took one of its underlying themes – the contrast between turbulent, violent Paris and safe, tranquil, and prosperous London. But Dickens' most obvious guide and inspiration was Carlyle. From him comes the lurid picture of a cruel and oppressive old order, a world of 'rapacious licence and oppression', where harmless and innocent victims can be confined by the whims of the powerful to years of imprisonment without trial in the grim and forbidding Bastille; where a nobleman can think the life of a child killed under the wheels of his coach can be paid for by a tossed gold coin. Worthless authorities rule over a wretched and poverty-stricken population aching with social resentment, in which Madame Defarge, impassively and implacably knitting, plans for the moment when revenge can be visited on her family's noble oppressors. The Revolution provides that moment: ' "The Bastille!" With a roar that sounded as if all the breath in France had been shaped into the detested word, the living sea rose, wave on wave, depth on depth, and overflowed the city to that point. Alarm bells ringing, drums beating, the sea raging and thundering on its own beach, the attack begun.' Madame Defarge helps to lead it: ' "What! We can kill as well as the men . . . !" And to her, with a shrill thirsty cry, trooping women variously armed, but all armed alike in hunger and revenge.' This turmoil goes on for years, but by 1792 the instrument of vengeance is the guillotine. Madame Defarge and her fellow Furies now knit around the scaffold, counting victims with their stitches. France is peopled with 'patriots in red caps and tricoloured cockades, armed with national muskets and sabres', sullen and suspicious, who instinctively curse all 'aristocrats'. 'That a man in good clothes should be going to prison, was no more remarkable than that a labourer in working clothes should be going to work.' By the beginning of 1794,

> Every day, through the stony streets, the tumbrils now jolted heavily, filled with the condemned. Lovely girls, bright women, brown-haired, black-haired, and grey; youths, stalwart men and old; gentle born and peasant born, all red wine for La Guillotine, all daily brought into light from the dark cellars of the loathsome prisons, and carried to her through the streets to slake her devouring thirst. Liberty, equality, fraternity, or death – the last, much the easiest to bestow, O Guillotine!

And although the French aristocrat Charles Darnay escapes, and his persecutor Madame Defarge is killed before she can pursue him, the book concludes with the English lawyer Sydney Carton sacrificing himself on the scaffold to her vengeance.

These images, intertwined with a powerfully crafted and heart-rending story, defined the French Revolution for Oscar Wilde's generation. For the next, and for the whole twentieth century, they were reinforced by the lesser talents of Mrs Montague Barstow, who dubiously capitalized on her birth in remote Hungary to call herself Baroness Orczy. *The Scarlet Pimpernel* (1905) and its later sequels chronicled the adventures of a foppish English knight, Sir Percy Blakeney, who led a double life rescuing innocent aristocrats from the guillotine by spiriting them, in various disguises, across the Channel to safety. But gone were the nuances found in Dickens. While the people of Paris remained 'a surging, seething, murmuring crowd, of beings that are human only in name, for to the eye and ear they seem naught but savage creatures, animated by vile passions and by the lust of vengeance and of hate', their victims, 'those aristos . . . all of them, men, women and children who happened to be descendants of the great men who since the Crusades had made the glory of France' were objects of pity, and in no way responsible for the supposed oppression of their ancestors. The whole episode was pure blood lust, successfully defied only by the efforts of 'that demmed elusive Pimpernel' and his intrepid band of secret agents, all English gentlemen. There is little hint in Orczy, unlike Carlyle or Dickens, that the old order had earned the fate that had befallen it. There is simply regret for 'beautiful Paris, now rendered hideous by the wailing of the widows, and the cries of the fatherless children'.

> The men all wore red caps – in various styles of cleanliness – but all with the tricolour cockade . . . their faces now invariably wore a look of sly distrust. Every man nowadays was a spy upon his fellows: the most innocent word uttered in jest might at any time be brought up as a proof of aristocratic tendencies, or of treachery against the people. Even the women went about with a curious look of fear and of hate lurking in their brown eyes, and all watched . . . and murmured . . . 'Sacrés aristos!'

## Twentieth-century parallels

*The Scarlet Pimpernel* began as a successful play, and was regularly re-adapted for stage and screen throughout the twentieth century. So was *A Tale of Two Cities*. The scope offered by both for costume drama was too rich for producers to resist for long. But for twentieth-century audiences seeking to sample revolution there were now more immediate examples. The Bolshevik Revolution in Russia in 1917, chronicled at once in language that echoed Carlyle by John Reed in *Ten Days that Shook the World* (1919), offered a fresh paradigm. It was also captured by the new and more immediate medium of film. Even more abundantly, so were subsequent upheavals in Germany, China, and countless other countries experiencing revolution in the later twentieth century. Figures like Lenin, Stalin, Hitler, and Mao have replaced Robespierre or Danton as quintessential revolutionaries in the popular imagination. Even the unique horror of the guillotine has been dwarfed by the gas chambers of the Holocaust, the organized brutality of the gulag, the mass intimidation of Mao's cultural revolution, or the killing fields of Cambodia. And yet many Russians in 1917 saw themselves, and indeed were widely seen, as re-enacting the struggles in France after 1789. Subsequent revolutionaries, if less conscious of the French precedents, have nevertheless sought legitimacy in doctrines of popular sovereignty all traceable to claims first explicitly made in 1789. Many, even those like the Nazis who professed to despise traditions now especially revered by Communism, celebrated their power with rituals and ceremonies redolent of the great set-piece festivals organized first in France between 1790 and 1794.

## The Corsican contribution

And one figure thrown up by the French Revolution has continued to be widely recognized – Napoleon. He remains one of the very few characters in history universally known by his first name, and by his appearance – especially if wearing his hat. He owes this recognition largely to remarkable achievements as a general, but his military prowess was built on the opportunities afforded him by the Revolution, and when he created new regimes In the aftermath of his victories, he thought it self-evident that they should run themselves on principles elaborated in France since 1789. Certainly, the nineteenth century was haunted by the memory of the way that he and the revolutionized French nation tore the rest of Europe (Great Britain excepted) apart. The Russians particularly, although they (or at least their climate) defeated him, were traumatized by the invasion of 1812. Half a century later, Tolstoy made the struggle against Napoleon the setting for *War and Peace* (1865–9). The novel's characters, from Czar Alexander downwards, are at the same time impressed and repelled by the Corsican usurper and what he stands for. For good or ill, he transforms all their lives. All the inhabitants of continental Europe during Napoleon's lifetime could have claimed as much. Even when he had gone, many of them found their everyday existence still regulated by laws which he had introduced. Napoleon claimed, when his campaigning days were over, that his most enduring glory would not be that of the battles he had won, but his Civil Code. In reality, the Code was a revolutionary project which Napoleon merely brought to fruition. But its impact was substantial enough, and not only in France. A simple, clear, and uniform set of principles for the holding and transfer of property, it remained the basis of civil law in much of Germany throughout the nineteenth century, in Poland until 1946, in Belgium and Luxembourg until the present day. Its influence still pervades the legal systems of Italy, the Netherlands, and Germany. An even greater success story has been metrication. Elaborated between 1790 and 1799, the decimal metric system of weights and measures was zealously promoted under Napoleon. Even in France it was slow to establish its monopoly, but in the subsequent two centuries it has spread to most of the world. When the United States succumbs, as sooner or later it surely will, it will mark the most complete triumph of any of the many trends and movements that the French Revolution began, its fullest and least ambiguous living legacy.

# CODE CIVIL

## DES
## FRANÇAIS.

ÉDITION ORIGINALE ET SEULE OFFICIELLE.

GRAND JUGE ET MINISTRE DE LA JUSTICE.

À PARIS,

DE L'IMPRIMERIE DE LA RÉPUBLIQUE.

An XII.    1804.

3. Enduring legacies: The Civil Code.

## DECLARATION OF THE RIGHTS OF MAN AND OF CITIZENS
### By the National Assembly of France

'THE Representatives of the people of France, formed into a National Assembly, considering that ignorance, neglect, or contempt of human rights, are the sole causes of public misfortunes and corruptions of Government, have resolved to set forth, in a solemn declaration, these natural, imprescriptible, and unalienable rights: that this declaration being constantly present to the minds of the members of the body social, they may be ever kept attentive to their rights and their duties: that the acts of the legislative and executive powers of Government, being capable of being every moment compared with the end of political institutions, may be more respected: and also, that the future claims of the citizens, being directed by simple and incontestible principles, may always tend to the maintenance of the Constitution, and the general happiness.

'For these reasons, the National Assembly doth recognize and declare, in the presence of the Supreme Being, and with the hope of his blessing and favour, the following sacred rights of men and of citizens:

I. Men are born, and always continue, free, and equal in respect of their rights. Civil distinctions, therefore, can be founded only on public utility.

II. The end of all political associations, is, the preservation of the natural and imprescriptible rights of man; and these rights are liberty, property, security, and resistance of oppression.

III. The nation is essentially the source of all sovereignty; nor can any individual, or any body of men, be entitled to any authority which is not expressly derived from it.

IV. Political Liberty consists in the power of doing whatever does not injure another. The exercise of the natural rights of every man, has no other limits than those which are necessary to secure to every other man the free exercise of the same rights; and these limits are determinable only by the law.

V. The law ought to prohibit only actions hurtful to society. What is not prohibited by the law, should not be hindered; nor should any one be compelled to that which the law does not require.

VI. The law is an expression of the will of the community. All citizens have a right to concur, either personally, or by their representatives, in its formation. It should be the same to all, whether it protects or punishes; and all being equal in its sight, are equally eligible to all honours, places, and employments, according to their different abilities, without any other distinction than that created by their virtues and talents.

VII. No man should be accused, arrested, or held in confinement, except in cases determined by the law, and according to the forms which it has prescribed. All who promote, solicit, execute, or cause to be executed, arbitrary orders, ought to be punished; and every citizen called upon, or apprehended by virtue of the law, ought immediately to obey, and renders himself culpable by resistance.

VIII. The law ought to impose no other penalties but such as are absolutely and evidently necessary: and no one ought to be punished, but in virtue of a law promulgated before the offence, and legally applied.

IX. Every man being presumed innocent till he has been convicted, whenever his detention becomes indispensible, all rigour to him, more than is necessary to secure his person, ought to be provided against by the law.

X. No man ought to be molested on account of his opinions, not even on account of his religious opinions, provided his avowal of them does not disturb the public order established by the law.

XI. The unrestrained communication of thoughts and opinions being one of the most precious rights of man, every citizen may speak, write, and publish freely, provided he is responsible for the abuse of this liberty in cases determined by law.

XII. A public force being necessary to give security to the rights of men and of citizens, that force is instituted for the benefit of the community, and not for the particular benefit of the persons with whom it is entrusted.

XIII. A common contribution being necessary for the support of the public force, and for defraying the other expences of government, it ought to be divided equally among the members of the community, according to their abilities.

XIV. Every citizen has a right, either by himself or his representative, to a free voice in determining the necessity of public contributions, the appropriation of them, and their amount, mode of assessment, and duration.

XV. Every community has a right to demand of all its agents, an account of their conduct.

XVI. Every community in which a separation of powers and a security of rights is not provided for, wants a constitution.

XVII. The right to property being inviolable and sacred, no one ought to be deprived of it, except in cases of evident public necessity, legally ascertained, and on condition of a previous just indemnity.'

Thomas Paine's translation into English from the French incorporated in his great attack on Burke, *Rights of Man* (1791)

## Human rights

'The Revolution was a grand thing!' exclaims Pierre Bezukhov in the first chapter of *War and Peace*. ' " . . . robbery, murder and regicide", . . . interjected an ironical voice. "Those were extremes, no doubt, but they are not what is most important. What is important are the rights of man, emancipation from prejudices, and quality of citizenship." Certainly this was what the Revolution began with, and on 26 August 1789 the National Assembly promulgated a founding manifesto to guide its work: the Declaration of the Rights of Man and the Citizen. This was something entirely new in the history of the world. The English Bill of Rights of 1689 had only proclaimed the rights of Englishmen. The United States did not establish its own Bill of Rights until a year after the French; and whereas the French declaration was meant as a preamble enshrining basic principles of a constitution, the American Bill was a series of afterthoughts, amendments to an already-existing constitution. Its principal architects, despite the precedent of declarations of rights prefacing a number of individual state constitutions in the 1770s, did not feel a properly drafted constitution was in need of what Alexander Hamilton, New York delegate to the Constitutional Convention, called 'aphorisms . . . which would sound much better in a treatise of ethics than in a constitution of government'.

A declaration of human rights was a hostage to fortune: but that is precisely what the French citizens of 1789 intended. Since 'ignorance, neglect, or contempt of human rights are the sole causes of public misfortunes and corruptions of Government', a statement of the 'natural, imprescriptible, and unalienable rights . . . constantly present to the minds of the members of the body social' would ensure that 'they may be ever kept attentive to their rights and their duties'. It would offer a yardstick against which all citizens could measure the behaviour of governments. Nor were these conceived of simply as French rights, although all French citizens were to enjoy them. Liberty, property, security, and resistance to oppression; civil equality, the rule of law, freedom of conscience and expression; the sovereign authority of nations and the answerability of governments to the citizenry; all these were declared human rights, and by implication applicable everywhere. It is true that within six years the French had redrafted this list twice, extending it and then restricting it. Napoleon abandoned it entirely in his successive constitutions. But every subsequent constitution-maker has felt obliged to make a principled decision about whether or not to incorporate such a declaration; and all those who have done so have gone back at some point to the prototype of 1789. When in 1948 the fledgling United Nations decided to adopt a Universal Declaration of Human Rights, the preamble and 14 out of its 30 articles were taken in substance, and sometimes in very wording, from the Declaration of 1789. Two further articles derived from the more ambitious Declaration of 1793, and one from the more modest Declaration of Rights and

Duties of 1795. The European Convention on Human Rights, adopted in 1953, was also full of the provisions and language of 1789. And, whereas France itself declined to ratify the European Convention until 1973, by the time of the bicentenary of the Revolution in 1989, President François Mitterrand had ordained that it should be celebrated as the Revolution of the Rights of Man.

## A disputed legacy

It was a vain hope. The British, as always, were determined to spoil France's party. Their royal family refused to attend any celebration of a regicide revolution. Margaret Thatcher declared that the rights of man were a British invention, and gave Mitterrand a lavishly bound copy of *A Tale of Two Cities*. A British historian working in America produced a vast chronicle of the Revolution which argued that its very essence was violence and slaughter (*Citizens*, by Simon Schama). It was a bestseller in a market where Burke, Carlyle, Dickens, and Orczy had clearly not laboured in vain. But even within France the celebrations proved bitterly contentious. Although when the Rights of Man were first proclaimed, the terror lay more than four years into the future, and the guillotine had not even been invented, few found it easy to look back on the Revolution as other than a single and consistent episode, for good or ill. For the left, the terror had been cruel necessity, made inevitable by the determination of the enemies of liberty and the rights of man to strangle them at birth. For the right, the Revolution had been violent from the start in its commitment to destroying respect and reverence for order and religion. Its logical culmination, some argued, was not merely terror, but, in the rebellious department of the Vendée, slaughter amounting to genocide. Many Catholic clergy, meanwhile, anathematized any celebration of what had brought the first attack in history on religious practice, using language that had scarcely changed in the course of two centuries. Mitterrand, however, enjoyed it all. The Revolution, he reflected with characteristic malice, 'is still feared, which inclines me rather to rejoice'.

A century, therefore, after thoughts of the French Revolution made Lady Bracknell shudder, people were still deeply divided about what 'that unfortunate movement' had led to. Everybody thought they knew, and few other historical episodes beyond living memory have remained capable of arousing such passionate admiration or loathing. That is because so many of the institutions, habits, attitudes, and reflexes of our own times can still be traced to what we think went wrong, or right, then. Greater knowledge of what occurred will not necessarily change anybody's mind. But it might offer a sounder basis for judgement than the random accumulation of snippets and snapshots which still satisfies most people's curiosity about this crossroads of modern history.

# Chapter 2
# **Why it happened**

We can scarcely discuss why anything happens until we have a basic
idea of what it is. Almost any attempt to define the French Revolution
too closely, however, will be tendentious, and exclude many of its
complexities. Yet what it most certainly was not, was a single event.
It was a *series* of developments, bewildering to most contemporaries,
which stretched over a number of years. It was a sustained period of
uncertainty, disorder, and conflict, reverberating far beyond the borders
of France. It began between 1787 and 1789.

## Financial overstretch

The crisis was triggered by King Louis XVI's attempts to avoid
bankruptcy. Over the eighteenth century, France had fought three
great wars on a worldwide scale. Accustomed by the pride, ambition,
and achievements of Louis XIV (1643–1715) to regarding herself as the
greatest European power, France found her pretensions challenged
over the three generations following the great king's death by the rise
of new powers – Russia, Prussia, and above all Great Britain. Rivalry
with the British was fought out on the oceans of the world. At stake
was dominance of the sources and supply of the tropical and oriental
luxuries for which Europe was developing an insatiable appetite.
Footholds in India, staging posts to China, fur-rich Canadian forests,
tropical islands where sugar and coffee could be produced, access to

supplies of slaves to work them: these were the prizes for which the British and French fought almost uninterruptedly throughout the 1740s and 1750s. But France also had land frontiers and traditional continental interests to defend, and in the mid-century wars Louis XV (1715–74) found his forces overextended on both land and sea. In the Seven Years War (1756–63) the results were disastrous. Despite alliances with Russia and even the traditional enemy Austria, his armies were humiliated by the upstart Prussians. At sea, the British destroyed both the Atlantic and Mediterranean fleets, drove French power out of India and North America, and all but strangled the trade of the French Caribbean. At the peace of Paris (1763), France made no European gains and lost Canada and most of her establishments in India. Not only was the defeat comprehensive and shameful, the war also left the kingdom burdened with a colossal debt which there was little prospect of diminishing, much less paying off. Servicing it absorbed 60 per cent of tax revenues. And yet almost at once a fresh naval build-up began, and when in the 1770s the colonists of British North America declared their independence, France saw the opportunity for revenge on the tyrant of the seas. The prospect of destroying the British Empire, and the commercial rewards that would result, seemed well worth a renewed effort, and in 1778 Louis XVI went to war to protect the fledgling United States. This time it was a spectacular success. While continental Europe remained at peace, France led a coalition against the isolated British which broke their control of the Atlantic long enough to ship a French army to America. When British forces surrendered at Yorktown in 1781, the victory was more French than American.

But France made no territorial gains when peace was signed in 1783, and the independent Americans gave no sign of abandoning their traditional British trading links. And meanwhile the war had been paid for largely by new loans rather than significant increases in taxation. In financial terms it ended not a moment too soon; but massive borrowing now continued into peacetime. By 1786 a foreseeable decline in tax revenues and the scheduled repayment of short-term war loans brought a financial crisis.

It was not that France lacked the resources to survive as a great power. Over the next generation the French would dominate the European continent more completely than they had ever done. It was rather that many of these resources were locked up by the system of government, the organization of society, and the culture of what revolutionaries would soon be calling the ancien régime, the old or former order. It took the Revolution to release them.

## The ancien régime: government

In political terms pre-revolutionary France was an absolute monarchy. The king shared his power with nobody, and was answerable for its exercise to nobody but God. Affairs of state, including the finances, were his private domain; and in all things he was sovereign in the sense that his decisions were final. On the other hand, no king was, or sought to be, a completely free agent. Even Louis XIV was careful to take advice on all important decisions, and men born to be king (for queens regnant were prohibited by French law) were carefully taught that counsel was of the essence of their sovereign authority. Louis XVI believed this implicitly; but unlike his grandfather Louis XV (his own father had died before inheriting the throne) he did not invariably do what a majority of his ministers recommended. He particularly thought he understood finance – a fateful delusion as it proved.

Nor was the king unfettered in his choice of advisers. Although he could sack them without explanation, his practical choice was limited to career administrators, magistrates, and courtiers. They, in turn, could only be brought to his notice by the intrigues of other ministers and familiars of both sexes drawn from the ranks or clienteles of the few hundred families rich enough to live in the gilded splendour of the Court. Imprisoned in scarcely changing routines of etiquette established in the previous century by Louis XIV, his two successors passed their lives peripatetically, following the hunting around forest palaces outside Paris – Fontainebleau, Compiègne, and of course Versailles, that spectacular seat of power imitated by rulers throughout Europe. When they visited the capital, it was briefly. Louis XIV had established this royal lifestyle deliberately to distance himself from a turbulent and volatile city whose people had defied royal authority during his minority in the uprising of the Fronde (1648–53). For their part, the Parisians remained suspicious and contemptuous of the Court. In 1789 many still remembered how, when celebrations in the capital to mark the future Louis XVI's marriage to the Austrian princess Marie-Antoinette in 1770 had led to a stampede in which 132 people were trampled to death, the festivities at Versailles had gone on regardless. Symbolizing the ill-starred alliance with the old enemy, the frivolous Marie-Antoinette never achieved popularity, even when, in 1781, she belatedly bore Louis XVI an heir. Her extravagance was so proverbial that even when rumours of it were disproved (as with her supposed secret purchase of a sumptuous diamond necklace in 1786) they were still believed. Unlike his raddled old grandfather, Louis XVI was a chaste family man who never took a mistress. But this threw the public spotlight onto his unpopular wife even more glaringly.

The king's absolute authority over the country at large was embodied in a handful of omnicompetent executive agents, the intendants. One of these was assigned to each of 36 generalities into which Louis XVI's kingdom was divided. The king thought them the showcase of his government, and there was no doubt about their high level of professionalism. But they were increasingly unpopular for their authoritarian ways, and their shortcomings and mistakes were mercilessly denounced by bodies whose authority they had largely supplanted since the seventeenth century. Taxation in some large provinces, for instance, still required the consent of estates – representative, though seldom elected, assemblies with no ultimate powers to resist, but whose semblance of independence enabled them to borrow relatively cheaply on the king's behalf. Above all, the fiscal and administrative work of the intendants was constantly impeded by the courts of law, most of which had administrative as well as judicial functions. At the summit of the judicial hierarchy sat the 13 parlements, supreme or 'sovereign' courts of appeal where registration was required for all important royal legislation before it became operative. Before registering, the parlements had the power to send the king remonstrances pointing out flaws or drawbacks in the new laws. Increasingly over the eighteenth century, remonstrances were printed and published, exposing the principles of monarchical government to public debate in a country where overt political discussion was deemed none of the subject's business. In the end, the king could override such protests, but the procedure, which involved the monarch or his representative coming to a court in person and supervising the transcription of contested measures into the judicial registers, was laborious and spectacular. It underlined the magistrates' recalcitrance as much as the king's authority.

As in every aspect of the ancien régime, the judicial and institutional map of France had no uniformity. Some of the parlements presided over small enclaves, others over extensive provinces. The jurisdiction of the parlement of Paris covered a third of the kingdom. But all of the 1250 members of these courts owned the offices they occupied, as a result of the practice of venality. Since the sixteenth century kings had systematically sold public offices, along with hereditary tenure or free disposal, as a way of borrowing for little outlay. By the eighteenth century there were perhaps 70,000 venal offices stretching far beyond the judiciary, but the prestigious core of the system was the 3200-strong nobility of the robe, whose judicial offices conferred ennoblement. Most prestigious among them were the magistrates of the parlements, and because dismissing them would have entailed reimbursing the value of their offices, they enjoyed virtually unchallengeable tenure. The king could bully them by shows of force, but without the money to buy them out, he could not dispossess them.

Accordingly, throughout the eighteenth century they were able to keep up a growing volume of criticism and obstruction against the crown's religious and financial policies. Only in 1771 did Louis XV's ministers feel able to promise any compensation for suppressed offices, and then the parlements were ruthlessly remodelled and muzzled. An opportunity was created for unobstructed reform, but Maupeou, the chancellor responsible, had no serious reforming intentions, and no advantage was taken. Meanwhile his attack on the parlements, which had increasingly come to be seen as the voice of the king's unrepresented subjects, proved hugely unpopular. Anxious to begin his reign in an atmosphere of confidence and popularity, the young Louis XVI was persuaded to dismiss Maupeou and restore them.

In the short run it worked. Although some provincial parlements remained fractious, and obstructed their local intendant more than ever, the crucially important parlement of Paris proved fairly pliable for the best part of a dozen years. It was, however, at the cost of the king attempting nothing too radical. Innovation was seen, and accepted even by most ministers, as dangerous. 'Any system', declared the parlement in remonstrances of 1776 against the replacement of forced labour on the roads with a tax,

> tending under the guise of humanity and benevolence to establish an equality of duties between men, and to destroy those distinctions necessary in a well-ordered monarchy, would soon lead to disorder . . . The result would be the overthrow of civil society, the harmony of which is maintained only by that hierarchy of powers, authorities, pre-eminences and distinctions which keeps each man in his place and keeps all Estates from confusion. This social order is not only essential to the practice of every sound government: it has its origin in divine law. The infinite and immutable wisdom in the plan of the universe established an unequal distribution of strength and character, necessarily resulting in inequality in the conditions of men within the civil order . . . These institutions were not formed by chance, and time cannot change them.

To abolish them, the whole French constitution would have to be overturned.

## The ancien régime: society

Yet it was hard to see how a French king could keep up his international pretensions without some modification in his subjects' time-honoured privileges and inequalities. Nowhere was the kingdom's lack of uniformity more glaring than in the structure of privilege and exemption which gave each and every institution, group, or area a status not quite like any other. The kingdom had been built up over many centuries by a gradual and often haphazard process of conquest and dynastic accumulation, and successive kings had won the obedience of their new subjects more by confirming their distinct institutions than by imposing a preferred pattern of their own. Ever since the sixteenth century these confusions had been compounded by the practice of selling privileges and exemptions (usually but not always as part of the sale of offices) as a roundabout way of borrowing. In earlier times it was easier to do than trying to force the rich to pay taxes. The most powerful groups in society, in any case, had elaborated persuasive rationales for exemption. The clergy, a vast corporation drawing revenues from a tenth of the kingdom's land, and creaming off, in the form of tithes, a notional tenth of the yield of the rest, paid no direct taxes on the grounds that it performed its service to society by praying and interceding with God. The nobility, the social elite which owned over a quarter of the land, levied feudal dues over much of the rest, and steadily sucked most of the newly rich into its ranks via ennobling offices, resisted the payment of direct taxes as well. Nobles, the argument went, served the kingdom with their blood, by fighting to defend it. Many did (though as officers only), but many more never drew the swords they wore to demonstrate their status. In any case these ancient arguments failed to keep the nobility exempt from new direct taxes introduced in and after 1695. Nevertheless, in most provinces, nobles continued to escape the oldest basic direct tax, the *taille*, not to mention forced labour on the roads. It was easy enough for rich commoners to buy themselves exemption as well, even if an ennobling office was beyond their means; simply moving to another town or province might be enough to secure real fiscal advantages. The burden of taxation, in other words, fell disproportionately on those least able to pay. To one extent or another, the rich were able to avoid it. It was the boast of the king's richest subject, his cousin the Duke d'Orléans, that he paid what he liked.

In real terms the total tax burden borne by the French had fallen over the eighteenth century. Yet whatever they paid they all considered themselves over-taxed. That was one reason why the resistance of the parlements, even though their magistrates were all nobles and represented nobody but themselves, was so popular. Even they recognized, however, that some emergencies necessitated higher taxes, and they acquiesced in a new levy of a twentieth on income from real estate in 1749. They even agreed to its doubling in 1756 and tripling in 1760. But the third twentieth lapsed when the Seven Years War ended, and meanwhile all sorts of provincial and institutional abatements had been negotiated, notably with the clergy and provinces retaining estates. Once assessments were established, the parlements always resisted their revision, even though this was an age of steady inflation. Their scepticism about the need for fiscal reform was only confirmed in the late 1770s when the American war was launched and sustained for four years without any substantial new taxation. This was the work of the Genevan banker Jacques Necker, who claimed to have achieved the incredible feat by 'economies' at the expense of courtiers and venal government financiers, two groups traditionally suspected of milking the public purse. But the purpose of such ostentatious savings was not to pay directly for the war, but to boost French credit in the international money market so as to sustain borrowing. Necker trumpeted his success in 1781 by publishing the first ever public statement of the royal accounts, the *Compte rendu au roi*. It showed the king's 'ordinary' accounts in modest surplus. It was what the public wanted to hear, and few cared that the massive 'extraordinary' expenditure, covered by loans raised on the credit of the ordinary surplus, went unmentioned. The longer term consequence was to undermine all attempts by Necker's successors to improve the kingdom's tax yield, especially once the war was over. If all had been well in 1781, people later asked, what had gone wrong since, and who was responsible?

Necker had been brought in more as a credit consultant than as a minister. As a foreign-born Protestant, in fact, he was legally ineligible for public office in a kingdom where Protestantism had not been recognized since 1685. But he soon learned that he could not impose financial discipline on ministers without the regular direct access to the king which their office gave them. When he attempted to use his popularity to force the king to admit him to his innermost counsels, however, Necker was rebuffed, and resigned. The gesture was unprecedented: one did not resign on the king of France. Nor had previous ex-ministers behaved as Necker now did, continuing to publish on financial affairs and orchestrating public criticism of the policies of his successors. What this outsider to the habits of absolute monarchy had grasped was that, in political as much as in financial affairs, public opinion, or what governments took it to be, was of ever-increasing importance; and that without public confidence even, and perhaps especially, the most absolute ruler could achieve very little.

## Public opinion

The constraints were obvious in innumerable ways. If, for instance, the whole financial history of the monarchy between 1720 and 1788 was a struggle to avoid bankruptcy, that was because renouncing debts, which earlier kings had done almost routinely, was no longer accepted as a legitimate option. Thousands had been ruined by a great financial crash in 1720, when another Protestant outsider, the Scotsman John Law, had attempted to liquidate the financial legacy of Louis XIV's wars by absorbing the accumulated debt into the capital of a commercial 'Royal Bank'. The collapse of this experiment also produced an enduring mistrust of banks and paper money despite all they had done in Holland or Great Britain to sustain an unprecedented war effort against France. For subsequent generations, any expedient which stirred such painful memories was generally regarded as unthinkable.

Kings who renounced their debts, or paid them in precarious paper rather than clinking coinage, were seen as conjuring irresponsibly with their subjects' property, behaving arbitrarily; whereas in French legal tradition royal authority was expected to observe the law, proceed by advice, and respect the rights and privileges of those whom God had entrusted to its care and protection. In the eighteenth century these expectations were reinforced by the widespread conviction that since nature herself (as Isaac Newton had shown) worked by invariable laws and not divine caprice, human affairs should also be conducted so far as was possible according to fixed and regular principles, rooted in rationality, in which the scope for arbitrariness was reduced to a minimum. Anything else, when a single individual governed, was despotism; which the most influential political writer of the century, Montesquieu had taught his compatriots to regard as the worst of all governments, where no law protected the subject from the ruler's whims. So that when a series of draconian debt consolidations in 1770, which many saw as a partial bankruptcy, was followed by Maupeou's attack on the parlements, despotism appeared to have struck. Traditional intermediary buffers between ruler and subject had been swept aside. And despite Louis XVI's restoration of the old parlements upon his succession, instinctive confidence in the traditional constitutional structure could never be fully revived.

Yet although the public saw no need for either higher taxes or bankruptcy, only a government strong and confident enough to attempt either was likely to be able to carry other reforms that had widespread support. The judiciary, for example, was perceived to be overstaffed, underemployed, and its procedures slow, expensive, and unreliable. A series of miscarriages of criminal justice exposed the cruelties and caprices of a system where magistrates were recruited by heredity or purchase rather than rational tests of competence. The labyrinthine complexities of the law, where attempts at codification had petered out in the 1670s, were sustained by innumerable local and provincial customs and privileges, many of them repeatedly confirmed in return for cash payments over the centuries. To reform any of this without compensating the losers would be widely seen as a breach of public faith, bankruptcy in disguise; but there was no prospect of ever finding the money to achieve it otherwise.

More thoughtful observers believed there were ways to square some circles. If economic productivity could be improved, fiscal benefits would be almost automatic. The Physiocrats or Economists (the first people to use this name) argued that all true wealth derived from agriculture, and that the land would produce more if natural laws were unimpeded by artificial human constraints. That implied tax reform – the abolition of burdensome charges like feudal dues in cash or kind, or tithes. It also meant commercial liberalization – the removal of controls on prices and free exchange, particularly in the grain trade. In comparison with agriculture, industry and commerce were held by these thinkers to be less important, and not generators of true wealth: but here too natural activity was impeded by over-regulation, the constraints imposed by trade guilds, and commercial monopolies. Administrators at every level found such reforming ideas increasingly attractive after mid-century; but as soon as they began to experiment with them they met with endless difficulties. Governments could not contemplate even the temporary loss of revenue, not to mention likely opposition from courts, estates, and various corporate bodies, which introducing a single tax would entail. Similarly with feudal dues: these were property rights, which could not be abolished equitably without compensation. A book advocating their suppression was publicly burned by order of the Paris parlement in 1776. As to the tithe, it was the main source of income of the parish clergy. Where would a substitute come from? The merest hint of commercial and industrial deregulation, meanwhile, was vigorously opposed by well-organized lobbies of merchants, chambers of commerce, and guild masters. Only in 1786 was trade with overseas colonies made completely free and open, and an attempt to abolish the monopolies of Parisian trade guilds ten years earlier was abandoned after only a few months of chaos. The only people, in fact, who could be subjected to the full force of Physiocratic policies were those too weak to resist: the king's poorest subjects. They bore the brunt of experiments from the 1760s onwards to deregulate the grain trade. The idea was to let prices rise to a 'natural' level. High prices, so the theory went, would encourage growers to increase production, and the end result would be 'abundance'. In the short term, however, higher grain prices meant dearer bread, especially when harvests were poor. The first experiments with deregulation, between 1763 and 1775, coincided with a series of such shortfalls; and as magistrates and local authorities had warned from the start, public order broke down as prices shot up and markets were bare. When ministers made agreements with contractors to guarantee emergency supplies, they were accused of a 'famine pact' to starve the people. In the weeks before Louis XVI's coronation in May 1775, popular goodwill was squandered by renewed deregulation and severe repression of the 'flour war' grain riots which followed. And although Necker, sniffing popularity as always, kept the trade firmly under control, his successors resumed tinkering. When, in 1788, the harvest failed completely, free export in previous years had denuded the kingdom of stocks. And the confidence of ordinary people that the king would protect them from starvation had been completely eroded by a generation of economic experiments at their expense.

Nor did they any longer expect much comfort from God's servants in the Church. While there was plenty of respect for underpaid parish priests and the selfless nuns who staffed hospitals and poorhouses, there was widespread disgust at the grotesque maldistribution of the Church's wealth, and the determination with which its richer beneficiaries defended their privileges. In mid-century the hierarchy had squandered much popular respect by zealous persecution of dissident priests who questioned authority in the Church in the name of Jansenism, an austere set of beliefs condemned as heretical by the papal bull *Unigenitus* of 1713. Jansenists were protected by sympathizers in the parlement of Paris, and in the 1740s and 1750s a series of lawsuits against priests refusing the last rites to dying Jansenists stirred up widespread fury against the hierarchy. When in 1757 Louis XV was (harmlessly) stabbed, his half-crazed assailant seemed to have acted out of vague sympathy for Jansenist tribulations. And Jansenism appeared to triumph in the 1760s when its oldest and most inveterate enemies, the Jesuits, found themselves involved in a case before the parlement. The magistrates used it as a pretext to expel them from the court's jurisdiction. Other parlements followed the lead, and a divided government acquiesced. The expulsion from the kingdom of a society which had educated most of the social elite for three centuries caused enormous educational upheaval. With the closure of their 106 colleges, something like a national curriculum was dissolved, and a generation of educational debate and experiment began. Almost at the same moment the establishment of a commission to review and consolidate failing monasteries suggested that even wider reform in the Church might be possible.

Educated critics had certainly been calling for it ever since the 1720s, when the scientific and humanistic development of the previous century began to crystallize into the utilitarian movement of criticism that came to be known as the Enlightenment. For the self-styled 'philosophers' who set out to popularize enlightened values, the established Church was the root of most of the evils in society. While the benevolent message of the Gospel was never disputed, clerics down the ages were deemed to have overlaid it with a mass of superstition and irrationality which they perpetuated through their influence in the state and control of the educational system. Happy to promote cruelty and intolerance, they had amassed disproportionate riches to support the idleness of unproductive monks and spendthrift chapters and prelates. Even the social services provided by the Church, such as poor relief and hospital care, were irrationally funded and inefficiently organized. These charges were pressed home with innuendo and ridicule, for which the mid-century quarrels within the Church provided plenty of material. The Church's response was to call for ever more vigorous and vigilant censorship, while attempting to reduce its own vulnerability by internal reforms such as the action on redundant monasteries. But neither approach restored confidence in an institution whose basic inertia, inflexibility, and self-satisfaction had alienated sympathy, in different ways, at every level of society.

In one sense, the Church was a victim of its own success. Nothing had done more over the century than the efforts of dedicated clerical teachers to increase levels of literacy from around a fifth of the population to nearer a third. More readers produced a rising demand for printed materials of all kinds. Book production soared; so did that of more ephemeral material like chapbooks, legal briefs sold for public consumption, and newspapers. By Louis XVI's time, Paris had a daily paper and most provincial towns had weeklies. It is true that they were mainly advertising sheets, and when they printed news it was largely without comment. But serious interest in public affairs could be gratified by a flourishing French-language press published abroad; and the cost of regular reading could be spread by joining one of the rapidly proliferating literary or reading societies whose libraries subscribed to all the major periodicals. Another indication of expanding demand for the printed word was the growth in the number of government censors to whom all substantial writings for the public had to be submitted; and the increasing amount of time and energy devoted by customs officials to blocking imports of subversive pornographic, blasphemous, or, as it was increasingly called, 'philosophical' literature. After a period in mid-century when ministers despaired of stemming the flood, and turned a blind eye to most of it, under Louis XVI the government redoubled its efforts to control what reached the reading public. But the market was too strong, and as much effort was soon being devoted to influencing what was reported and discussed as to preventing its appearance. Louis XIV had told his subjects what to do, and what to think. Under Louis XVI, it was recognized that they had to be persuaded.

The virtues of active cooperation between kings and their subjects had long been displayed across the Channel. Ever since the 1720s writers like Montesquieu and Voltaire had extolled the enabling freedoms of British liberty, toleration, and parliamentary government. British success in mid-century wars had shown that the system, still suspect to many for its dangerous volatility, was also formidably efficient. Some of the gloss was taken from the image of Great Britain when her colonies rebelled, and Anglomania was partially eclipsed by enthusiasm for all things American. But liberty and political representation were at the heart of the Anglo-American quarrel; and when Louis XVI allied with republican rebels who had proclaimed no taxation without representation, his subjects could scarcely help reflecting on why this principle was not deemed appropriate in France. In the handful of provinces with estates, of course, it was; but that made the situation elsewhere seem even more anomalous. As fiscal pressures increased, certain magistrates in the 1760s began to call for lost estates to be restored. When Maupeou attacked the parlements in 1771, some went further and called for a meeting of the nearest French equivalent to the British parliament, the medieval Estates-General, last convened in 1614. Others, with the comfortable ambiguities of absolute monarchy now exposed as empty, began to think of more rationally designed representative institutions that would visibly involve taxpayers in administration. Nor were ministers necessarily opposed to a principle which might sideline the parlements and their influence. Necker even began a programme of introducing 'provincial administrations', nominated assemblies of local landowners who would share the functions of intendants. Only two were established before his resignation, but they did not disappear with him. Slowly, hesitantly, with many misgivings but aware that

Why it happened

institutional paralysis was the only alternative, the monarchy was becoming less absolute under Louis XVI. The king and his ministers increasingly recognized that France must be governed with the effective consent and cooperation of the crown's most prominent and educated subjects.

## The 'Pre-Revolution'

So the crisis of 1787 was not just financial. Calonne, the finance minister appointed in 1783 to manage a return to peacetime conditions, began with lavish expenditures in the hope of sustaining confidence. The borrowing which this required achieved just the reverse. As attempts to float new loans ran into increasing resistance in the Paris parlement, Calonne turned his thoughts to more radical solutions. On 20 August 1786 he presented the king with a comprehensive plan of reform, later described by the courtier bishop Talleyrand as 'more or less the result of all that good minds have been thinking for several years'. The king, after considering it carefully, accepted it with genuine enthusiasm.

The plan was threefold. First came fiscal reform, in the guise of a new, uniform land tax, with no exemptions, to be levied in kind. This, and other less important innovations, were to be overseen throughout the kingdom by provincial assemblies elected by all prominent landowners. Representative government was to be universalized – though not centralized in a national assembly. Secondly, the fiscal yield of the reforms was to be boosted by a programme of economic stimulation on Physiocratic lines: abolition of internal customs barriers, of forced labour on the roads, and of controls over the grain trade. In 1786, a commercial agreement with Great Britain had already opened French markets to British manufacturers in exchange for agricultural products. None of these measures, however, could be expected to yield immediate benefits. More borrowing would be required until the effects were felt. A major new boost in confidence was therefore required to encourage lenders. Calonne hoped to achieve this by having his plans endorsed by a handpicked Assembly of Notables, people (as he put it) 'of weight, worthy of the public's confidence and such that their approbation would powerfully influence general opinion'. He considered convoking the Estates-General, but thought them likely to be uncontrollable. Instead he nominated 144 princes, prelates, noblemen, and magistrates, before whom he laid his proposals in February 1787.

It was a political disaster. Few of the Notables accepted Calonne's version of the crisis confronting the state. Even those who did tended to hold him responsible, and therefore not the right person to resolve it. An attempt by Calonne to appeal over his critics' heads to the wider public, by depicting them as mere selfish defenders of their own privileges, backfired; and the king was forced to dismiss him. An amended version of his plan was then brought forward by Brienne, an archbishop who had used the Notables as a ladder to power. It got nowhere when Louis XVI refused the Notables' proposal for a permanent commission of auditors to vet the royal accounts. By now, in fact, growing numbers in the assembly were declaring themselves incompetent to sanction reform of any sort. That, they declared, required nothing less than the Estates-General.

Experience with the Notables only made this seem more dangerous and unpredictable than ever, and on 25 May the assembly was dissolved. An attempt was now made to push the reforms through the parlements, but they too claimed incompetence. As crowds came onto the streets to cheer for the Estates-General, the Parisian magistrates were sent into exile. The wider significance of the crisis was underlined meanwhile in the Dutch Republic, which was overrun by a Prussian invasion in mid-September. Louis XVI had threatened to intervene if Dutch territory was violated; but, with old taxation running out and new unauthorized, Brienne advised him that he could not afford to. It was the end of the Bourbon monarchy as a military power; an admission that, even close to its own frontiers, it could no longer pay for its international pretensions.

Within a year its domestic political authority had also evaporated. Attempts to engineer a consensual reform plan with the Paris parlement collapsed amid suspicious recriminations, and for six months the sovereign courts refused to transact business. In May 1788, a Maupeou-like attempt was made to remodel them and reduce their powers. To win public support a wide range of legal and institutional reforms were simultaneously announced, but they were ignored in the public uproar that now swept the country. Even a promise to convoke the Estates-General once the reforms had taken effect was greeted with contempt. And when, at the beginning of August, the crown's usual sources of short-term credit refused to lend more, the fate of Brienne's ministry was sealed. On 16 August, payments from the treasury were suspended. It was the bankruptcy which successive ministries had spent 30 years trying to avoid. Brienne resigned, recommending the recall of Necker. The first thing the Genevan miracle-worker did on his triumphant return to office was to proclaim that the Estates-General would meet in 1789.

The convocation of a national representative assembly meant the end of absolute monarchy. It had finally succumbed to institutional and cultural paralysis. Its plans for reform fell with it. Nobody knew what the Estates-General would do, or even how it would be made up or chosen. There was a complete vacuum of power. The French Revolution was the process by which this vacuum was filled.

# Chapter 3
# **How it happened**

A month before monarchical authority collapsed into bankruptcy, a
colossal hailstorm swept across northern France and destroyed most
of the ripening harvest. With reserves already low after Calonne had
authorized free export of grain in 1787, the inevitable result was that
the months before the harvest of 1789 would bring severe economic
difficulties. Bread prices would rise, and as consumers spent more
of their incomes on food, demand for other goods would fall.
Manufactures, hit by cheaper British competition under the
commercial treaty of 1786, were already slumping; and there were
widespread layoffs at the very time when bread prices began to soar.
On top of all this came an unusually cold winter, when rivers froze,
immobilizing mills and bulk transport and producing widespread
flooding when a thaw finally came. So the political storm that was about
to break would take place against a background of economic crisis, and
would be profoundly affected by it.

## Electoral politics

Necker moved quickly on returning to office to reimpose controls on
the grain trade. It was too late, but the gesture only added to his
phenomenal popularity. He needed it all to deal with other problems.
The most pressing was the form to be taken by the Estates-General. One
of Brienne's last acts had been to declare that the king had no fixed view

on the question. To the parlement of Paris this seemed to imply a desire to rig the assembly in advance; and to prevent any such move the magistrates declared on 25 September that the Estates-General should be constituted in the same way as when they had last met, according to the forms of 1614. Well-informed observers realized at once that this was a recipe for prolonging the institutional paralysis which had brought down absolute monarchy. In 1614, the Estates-General had sat in three separate orders, representing clergy, nobility, and the third estate – meaning everybody else. They had voted by order, so any two could outvote a third. Such a distribution of powers and representation no longer reflected the realities of education, wealth, and property as they had developed over the eighteenth century; and a thoughtful group of Parisians, mostly noblemen, set out in a so-called 'committee of thirty' to arouse public opinion against it. They flooded the excited country with pamphlets, and their efforts were only lent strength when a reconvened Assembly of Notables rejected Necker's urgings and rallied behind the forms of 1614. The Notables' caution looked, or was made to look, like a bid for power by the old 'privileged orders' at the expense of the vast majority of the nation. For the first time since the beginning of the crisis in 1787, the politics of social antagonism began to dominate public debate. 'What is the Third Estate?' asked the title of the most celebrated pamphlet of that winter, by the renegade clergyman Sieyès, 'Everything. What has it been until now in the public order? Nothing. What does it want to be? Something.' Anyone laying claim to any sort of privilege, Sieyès went on to argue, excluded themselves by that very fact from the national community. Privileges were a cancer.

By December the clamour against the forms of 1614 was so well established that Necker felt emboldened to act. He decreed that, in recognition of their weight in the nation, the number of third-estate deputies would be doubled. It was obvious that this meant little if voting was still to be by order rather than by head, but Necker believed that the clergy and nobility could be induced to renounce the privilege for themselves once the Estates-General met. He relied on general dissatisfaction with the half-measure of doubling the third to dominate the elections of the spring of 1789 to such a degree that resistance to uniting the orders would become unthinkable. Vote by head was indeed one of the central preoccupations of the electoral assemblies; but since they too were separate, with each order electing its own deputies, the effect was to polarize matters still further. In the face of tumultuous popular support for third-estate aspirations, clerical and noble electors tended to see their privileges as an essential safeguard of their identity; and most of those they elected to represent them were intransigents. Opinion was crystallized further on all sides by the process of drafting *cahiers* (grievance lists which were also part of the forms of 1614) to guide the deputies chosen. Now emerged questions not only of how the estates were to be constituted, but of what they were actually to do. An amazing range of grievances and aspirations were articulated in what amounted to the first public opinion poll of modern times. Suddenly changes seemed possible that only a few months earlier had been the stuff of dreams; and the tone of the *cahiers* made clear that many electors actually expected them to happen through the agency of the Estates-General.

## National sovereignty

But when the Estates-General met at Versailles on 5 May they proved a massive disappointment. Necker opened proceedings with a boring speech, and from the start the third-estate deputies made clear that they would transact no business as a separate order. Their calls to the nobility and clergy to unite with them, however, fell on deaf ears. Even the small number of noble deputies who favoured deliberation and voting in common refused to break ranks. The stalemate continued for six weeks, during which bread prices continued to rise, public order began to break down in many districts, and the widespread hopes of the spring began to turn sour. Eventually, on 10 June, Sieyès proposed that the third estate 'cut the cable' and begin proceedings unilaterally. After an overwhelming vote in favour, they invited the other orders to verify credentials in common, and three days later a handful of parish priests broke the solidarity of the privileged orders to answer the invitation. Other clergy trickled in over the next few days, and a body that was no longer just representative of the third estate recognized that it now needed a new name. Once again at Sieyès' instigation, on 17 June it chose an obvious but uncompromising title: the National Assembly. Immediately afterwards it decreed the cancellation and then re-authorization of all taxes. The implication was clear. This assembly had seized sovereign power in the name of the French Nation.

It was the founding act of the French Revolution. If the Nation was sovereign, the king no longer was. Louis XVI, shaking off the grief which had paralysed him since the death of his elder son a few days before, now declared that he would hold a Royal Session to promulgate a programme of his own. Locked out of its usual meeting place by preparations for this, the suspicious self-proclaimed National Assembly convened on 20 June in an indoor tennis court and took an emotional oath never to separate until they had given France a constitution. The first test of the deputies' resolution came three days later at the Royal Session when the king, after announcing a number of concessions, quashed all the claims made between 10 and 17 June, and instructed the orders to reconvene separately. They refused; and, flustered by news that Necker had resigned, the king let them stay. By now Versailles was filled daily with restive crowds from Paris. Aware that they could no longer rely on support from the throne, noble and clerical separatists found their solidarity crumbling. Soon they were joining the National Assembly in droves, and on 27 June the king formally ordered the last diehards to do so. Necker withdrew his resignation. The royal surrender seemed complete.

Unknown to Necker, however, and perhaps at first to the king himself, ministerial orders had been issued on 26 June to certain regiments to converge on Versailles. More were ordered up in the weeks that

4. 20 June 1789: The Tennis Court Oath. The National Assembly vows never to disperse until it has given France a constitution.

followed, and by early July the nervous Assembly was importuning the king to withdraw the troops. He replied, plausibly enough, that their presence was necessary to secure public order; but when on 12 July Necker was dismissed more sinister suspicions seemed borne out. The 20,000 soldiers now encamped around the Île de France appeared poised to overawe the capital while action was taken to subdue the Assembly. On hearing the news about Necker, Paris exploded with a mixture of fear and indignation. Tentative moves by German mercenary troops to disperse crowds only made things worse, and members of the permanent Paris garrison of French Guards began to desert. Soon bands of hungry insurgents were ransacking strongpoints in the city for arms, powder, and hoards of flour. On 14 July they converged on the massive state prison of the Bastille, which commanded the entire east end of the city with its guns. With the help of military deserters, they stormed the prison and forced its surrender, massacring the commander who had fired on them early in the attack. Paris was now in rebel hands. There were certainly enough troops surrounding the city to subdue the revolt, but commanders advised the king that they might not obey orders to shoot. In these circumstances he was powerless, and ordered a withdrawal. A counter-revolution had been defeated. The National Assembly had been saved.

## The first reforms

The 14 July was not, therefore, the beginning of the French Revolution. It was the end of the beginning. Nor did the opening of the grim and mysterious Bastille release the expected host of languishing victims of despotism. There were only seven prisoners. But the medieval fortress was a symbol of royal power, and the spontaneous demolition of it which began at once was equally symbolic of the end of a discredited old order. Those who had orchestrated royal resistance over the month since 17 June recognized the situation, too: the king's brother Artois and his closest courtier friends left the country at once, the first émigrés. After the king had been to Paris and, accepting the new tricolour

42

5. 14 July 1789: The taking of the Bastille.

cockade of revolution from a hastily formed citizens' militia (soon to be called the National Guard), confirmed a self-appointed municipal administration, the National Assembly at last began work on the constitution to which it had committed itself in the tennis court oath. Binding mandates imposed by electors in the spring were abrogated, and a preamble to the constitution, a declaration of rights, began to be drafted. But by now upheavals in Paris and certain provincial cities had spread to the countryside, where the weeks before the new harvest ripened were marked by a 'great fear' that 'brigands' were scouring the land to destroy crops and pillage helpless peasant communities. In this paranoid atmosphere there were widespread attacks on the houses of lords and the symbols of feudal power, which, as the *cahiers* had shown, peasants regarded as the least justifiable of the many burdens they bore. The men of property who made up the Assembly, whether owners of feudal rights or not, were genuinely alarmed that the country was collapsing into anarchy. To defuse the chaos, a radical group planned a dramatic gesture in which feudal dues would be abolished. It was launched by a great nobleman on the evening of 4 August, and was greeted with a rush of enthusiasm in an Assembly that had impatiently held back from positive action for much of the three months of its existence. Soon more than feudal rights were proposed for abolition. All sorts of privileges, the very lifeblood of ancien régime social organization, were grandiloquently renounced. So was venality of offices, from which many privileges had derived. Free justice was proclaimed, and equality of taxation. The Church was deprived of tithes, the basic income of the parish clergy. By the end of the session, when the Assembly declared the king 'Restorer of French Liberties' much of the fabric of French social life had been condemned to destruction in the most radical few hours of the entire Revolution.

As several of those present observed, there had been a sort of magic in the air that night: but the magic worked. Gradually rural disorder subsided. The Assembly (now calling itself the National Constituent

Assembly) returned to its constitution-making. On 26 August it finally promulgated a Declaration of the Rights of Man and the Citizen, and over subsequent weeks it established the first principles of a constitutional monarchy, ruling out a bicameral legislature and granting the king limited powers of veto on new laws. The king, however, seemed in no hurry to accept this restriction, or indeed any of the great measures enacted in August. Suspicions aroused in July now began to fester anew in Paris, whose populace clearly regarded themselves as the saviours and watchdogs of the Revolution. When, early in October, new military arrivals were reported from Versailles by a Parisian press now free and constantly proliferating, fear spread that the king was about to attempt again what had failed in the summer. Sweeping aside attempts by the National Guard to restrain them, thousands of women marched on Versailles to coerce the king. There they invaded the hall of the Assembly, broke into the palace, and threatened the life of the queen. The only thing that would satisfy them, they eventually clamoured, was for the royal family to come with them to Paris. The monarch quickly saw that he had little choice, and on 6 October he was escorted back to his capital by the triumphant women. The Assembly followed a few days later.

## Polarization: religion

Louis XVI was now the prisoner of Paris. Apart from an ill-fated attempt to escape in June 1791, he would remain so until the monarchy was overthrown in August 1792. So, however, would the Assembly. Although the deputies knew that they probably owed their survival to Parisian popular action, most of them remained deeply uneasy about the obligation. That was shown by their enactment of a martial law against tumults, and by the way they confined political rights under the constitution to substantial taxpayers. Their aim was to set up a constitutional monarchy controlled by the elected representatives of substantial men of property. Their commitment to property owners was also shown in their refusal to renounce the debt bequeathed by absolute monarchy, and indeed a massive expansion of it by promises to compensate all those, such as venal office-holders, whose property would disappear as a result of their reforms. They soon saw that all this could not possibly be met out of taxation. Tax revenues, in fact, were falling catastrophically in the absence of any effective means of coercion. Their solution was to satisfy the nation's creditors at the expense of the Church.

By the abolition of tithe on 4 August the Assembly had already committed itself to ecclesiastical reform. Finding an alternative source of income for the parish clergy was not the least of the new obligations it had taken on. But the Church remained rich in lands and endowments and already on 4 August isolated voices had claimed that the rightful owner of these assets was the Nation. On 2 November it was decided to place them 'at the disposal of the Nation'. They were to be sold to support an issue of state bonds, called *assignats*, in which other public debts would be redeemed. To many clergy and devout laity these measures looked like part of a wider attack on the Catholic faith. Amid triumphant invocations of the philosophers who had attacked the Church throughout the eighteenth century, the Assembly proclaimed civil equality for Protestants and prohibited monastic vows. When urged in April 1790 to declare Catholicism the state religion, it refused; and by then civil strife had broken out between Catholics and Protestants in the south, around Nîmes. Finally, given that the Nation was now to pay the clergy out of public funds, the Assembly decided to reorganize the Church in accordance with the same broad principles it was applying to the country at large. And so the civil constitution of the clergy, enacted in July 1790, provided for lay election of priests and bishops, nationalization of ecclesiastical boundaries, and a purely honorific role for the pope – who as a foreign ruler was not consulted on any of these principles. Nor were the clergy themselves, which left many of them uncertain whether such a radical reorganization was acceptable to the Church as a whole. The Assembly saw their hesitation as a deliberate obstruction of the national will, and in November imposed an oath of obedience on all clergy. 'Refractories' who refused it were to be ineligible for benefices under the new order.

They expected that to settle matters; but in fact only around half of the clergy complied. Many retracted when in the spring of 1791 the pope publicly denounced the civil constitution. It was the beginning of the first, deepest, and most persistent polarization of the Revolution. As revolutionary 'patriots' mobilized to promote compliance with the oath, producing a massive expansion of the political 'Jacobin' clubs that had begun to be established over the previous winter, counter-revolutionaries were quick to associate their own cause with threatened Christianity. Acceptance of the sacraments from a 'constitutional' priest who had taken the oath became a touchstone of loyalty to the entire Revolution. No sincere Catholic could evade this decision; and this included the king.

## Polarization: monarchy

After his return to Paris, Louis XVI had grudgingly accepted all the reforms of the Constituent Assembly, with occasional displays almost of enthusiasm. He even sanctioned the ecclesiastical legislation, although he privately knew of the pope's hostility. It was soon obvious in the spring of 1791, however, that he was avoiding receiving the sacraments from constitutionals. Threatening demonstrations began to occur around the Tuileries palace, for in Paris there was overwhelming support for oath-taking. This renewed popular hostility determined the royal family to attempt escape. On the night of 20 June they slipped out of Paris, making for the eastern frontier. The king imprudently left behind him an open letter denouncing much of the work of the Revolution. But the fugitives were captured at Varennes, and brought back to Paris in disgrace.

The flight to Varennes opened up the second great schism of the Revolution. There had been hardly any republicanism in 1789, and what

47

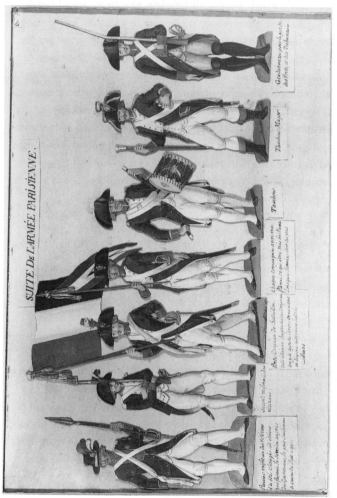

6. National Guards in uniform, with the tricolour.

there was abated once the king was back in Paris and accepting all the Assembly sent him. But, after Varennes, the mistrust built up by his long record of apparent ambivalence burst out into widespread demands from the populace of the capital and a number of radical publicists for the king to be dethroned. Most members of the Assembly, however, were horrified, conniving hastily at the obvious official lie that the keystone of their constitution had been abducted. When the Paris Jacobin club flirted with a republican petition, most deputies seceded from it to form a more moderate 'Feuillant' club; and when crowds gathered in the great military parade ground to the west of the city, the Champ de Mars, to sign the same petition National Guards opened fire on them. The Assembly decided that the constitution must now be quickly finished, and revised at the same time to make it more acceptable to the king, so that normal political life could begin. After hurried changes to exclude religious clauses and limit the freedom of the press and of political clubs, the constitution of 1791 was presented to the king who, having publicly accepted it, was officially reinstated. On the last day of September, the Constituent Assembly came to an end, its members having formally disqualified themselves from sitting in the Legislative Assembly that was now to assume power.

The Legislative Assembly met in an atmosphere of international crisis. For the first time since 1787, the flight to Varennes had made French affairs a subject of concern rather than disdainful satisfaction to foreign powers. In May 1790 the Constituent Assembly had positively renounced war as an instrument of policy, except in self-defence. But after the ignominious recapture of a king who appeared bent on internationalizing his plight, other monarchs were alarmed. In the Declaration of Pillnitz (27 August 1791) the Emperor and the king of Prussia were induced by Louis XVI's two émigré brothers, Artois and Provence, to threaten military intervention. Thousands of army officers had joined the émigrés after Varennes, and were now massing across the frontier dreaming of a return with foreign armies. The king and queen shared these dreams; but the new deputies saw them as a provocation. Over the autumn and winter their language became hysterically belligerent towards the German princelings who harboured the émigrés and, behind them, the Habsburg Emperor. They also sought to provoke Louis XVI into compromising himself by passing decrees intensifying penalties against refractory priests and émigrés which they knew he would not sanction. General paranoia was intensified by news of a massive slave uprising in the Caribbean, and the coffee and sugar shortages that followed. Despite fears, evinced by Jacobins like Robespierre, that the debilitated army was in no state to defeat the disciplined forces of Austria and Prussia, most of the country was carried away by war fever. The king (who shared Robespierre's analysis but saw it as a sign of hope for his own rescue) was therefore happy to declare war on the Emperor on 20 April 1792.

## Polarization: war

War was the third great polarizing issue of the Revolution. As was intended, it forced everybody to take sides on everything else. It identified the defeat or survival of the Revolution with that of the nation itself, so that critics of anything achieved since 1789 could be plausibly stigmatized as traitors. Most vulnerable to this charge was the king himself, who persisted in his vetoes of laws against refractories and émigrés despite being mobbed in his palace on 20 June by Parisians now calling themselves sansculottes. No doubt his resolution was steeled by news of disasters from the front, as Prussia entered the war and prepared to invade French territory. Even French generals called for peace negotiations. But this too looked like little less than treason, and the Assembly decreed the reinforcement of the line army by National Guard volunteers (*fédérés*). As they began to arrive in Paris, those from Marseilles singing a new and bloodthirsty battle hymn that would forever afterwards bear their name, the Prussian commander threatened to destroy Paris if the king was harmed. That completed the identification of Louis XVI with the enemy, and on 10 August an insurrectionary commune of Paris launched a force of sansculottes and *fédérés* against the royal palace. The king took refuge with the Assembly while his Swiss life-guards were massacred defending his empty residence; but this did not save his throne. The Assembly voted to suspend the monarchy and convoke a new body elected by manhood suffrage, the Convention, to draw up a republican constitution for the country.

The full impact and implications of the overthrow of monarchy took the rest of the year to become manifest. Meanwhile the Prussians pushed into France, and Paris remained panic-stricken. A provisional executive council dominated by the Parisian demagogue Danton frenziedly attempted to organize defence with a series of draconian emergency powers which filled the prisons with suspects. As patriotic sansculottes were urged to join up, anxiety spread about a possible prison breakout in their absence. On 2 September, as news arrived that the Prussians had captured Verdun, prisons were broken into and their inmates taken out and massacred. The carnage went on for four days, leaving about 1400 victims dead, among them many refractory priests. Although the inflammatory populist journalist Marat urged provincial France to follow the capital's example, news of the massacres horrified opinion both in France and abroad. This was something altogether more serious than the occasional lynchings of 1789 and since, a grim lesson of what happened if the lower orders were not kept under control. Enemies of the Revolution had always predicted bloody chaos; those who wished it well mostly found the massacres equally hard to justify. Everybody in Paris, however, lived henceforth in the fear that they might very well happen again.

And yet within weeks the crisis seemed to be over. On the day before the Convention replaced the Legislative, a French army confronted the Prussian invaders at Valmy and defeated them (20 September). It was the beginning of six months of brilliant military success in which the Austrian Netherlands and the left bank of the Rhine were overrun. By November, intoxicated by the apparent ease of their success, the French

51

were offering 'Fraternity and help to all peoples wishing to recover their liberty' and 'war on the castles, peace to the cottages' in the path of their armies. They promised to implement revolutionary social policies wherever they went, and make churches and nobles pay for the process. 'We cannot be calm', declared the journalist deputy Brissot, consistently the leading advocate of war since October 1791, 'until Europe, all Europe, is in flames.' The challenge was compounded by the fate of Louis XVI. The first act of the Convention was to declare the monarchy abolished. Later it would retrospectively date a new republican calendar from this moment, the Year I of Liberty. That left the question of what to do with 'Louis Capet' or 'Louis the Last'. When it was argued that he should be put on trial for crimes against the nation, some argued that his very overthrow by the populace constituted a trial and guilty verdict. But a trial before the Convention was eventually agreed, the indictment covering the king's whole record since 1789. It took less than two days in December, and despite the defendant's denial of all the charges, there was never any doubt what the verdict would be. Only the sentence was contentious, a decision to execute him passing by a single vote. There were also unsuccessful proposals to subject the result to a referendum, and to grant clemency. But the majority knew that the watching sansculottes would probably not have allowed either; and so on 21 January 1793 the former king went to public execution. 'You have thrown down your gauntlet', Danton exulted in the Convention, 'and this gauntlet is a king's head!'

## Civil war and terror

The challenge was soon taken up. Within days of the execution Great Britain and the Dutch Republic joined the Republic's enemies, soon followed by Spain and several Italian states. When the Convention sought to augment its armed forces by conscripting 300,000 new recruits, there was widespread resistance across the west of the country, where the persecution of refractory priests had already caused rioting. In the Vendée, south of the Loire, civil war was soon raging, with

7. 21 January 1793: The execution of Louis XVI. Note the vacant pedestal where his grandfather's statue had previously stood.

the rebels organizing themselves into a self-styled 'Catholic and Royal Army' dedicated to restoring the heirs of the martyred king. Now, too, the war against the Republic's foreign enemies began to go badly. French forces were driven out of the Rhineland and Belgium, where their general deserted to the enemy. The crisis exacerbated long-standing political divisions within the Convention. The advocates of open-ended war, led by Brissot and a number of Bordeaux deputies whom Robespierre called the 'faction of the Gironde' thought that it could and should be conducted without compromising the Revolution's original and representative principles at home. It was they who sought national endorsement of the judgements against the king. And, in the wake of the September massacres, the Girondins argued loudly against the intimidation of the Convention's proceedings by the bloodstained populace of Paris. These stances won them expulsion from the Jacobin club, whose leaders, such as Robespierre, were soon called Montagnards (literally 'mountain men', from the high benches they occupied in the Convention). Montagnards, apart from personal dislike, thought the Girondins' vendetta against Paris suicidally distracting from more practical priorities. They saw no safe alternative to humouring the sansculottes, even if that meant turning a blind eye to their more violent instincts and excesses. By May, with bad news arriving from all sides, they had concluded that the only way to silence the Girondins was to accept sansculotte demands for their expulsion from the Convention. On 2 June, 29 of them were arrested.

The immediate effect was only to intensify the crisis. Already restive at their inability to influence events in Paris, several provincial cities now came out into open revolt. Over the summer, Marseille, Bordeaux, and Lyon were beyond the Convention's control, and at the end of August the great Mediterranean naval port of Toulon surrendered to the British. On 13 July, meanwhile, Marat, the journalistic idol of the sansculottes, was assassinated in his bath by Charlotte Corday, an insurgent from Caen. Much of this so-called 'Federalist Revolt' was not counter-revolutionary in the way the Vendée uprising quite explicitly was. It was a protest against extremism and instability in the capital. But rebellion, however motivated, in time of war was undoubtedly treasonable; and as, over the autumn, the Convention's forces re-established control over centres which proved unable to coordinate their efforts, rebel leaders and activists paid the traitors' penalty. Almost 14,000 were sentenced to death by special courts in the provinces over the autumn and winter. Over half were in the west, where the last Vendéan army was defeated in December. Some were shot or drowned, but most died under the instrument that had dispatched the king, the guillotine – introduced only in April 1792 and designed as a humane means of execution by rational men who failed to foresee the effect of the rivers of blood it released when used on large numbers of victims.

The aim of such retribution was as much to terrorize as to punish; and by September the sansculottes, unable to understand why the elimination of their legislator enemies had not produced more positive results, were pressing for terror to be adopted as a principle of government. Intimidated once more by mass demonstrations on 5 September, the Convention declared terror the order of the day. Within a few weeks it had decreed the arrest of all suspects, expanded a revolutionary tribunal established earlier in the year to try political crimes, imposed price controls on all basic commodities (the 'maximum'), and authorized so-called 'revolutionary armies' of sansculottes to force peasants to disgorge their surpluses to feed the cities. The government of the Republic was now to be 'revolutionary until the peace' – centralized, arbitrary, and armed with emergency powers, all the very opposite of the constitutional conduct of affairs to which the Revolution had committed itself from the outset.

Now the Girondins arrested in June, and the hated widow of Louis XVI, Marie-Antoinette, were sent to the scaffold, for what they symbolized as much as for what they had done. A number of deputies, dispatched to disturbed provinces as 'representatives on mission' and invested with the full powers of the Convention also began to identify, reasonably enough in many cases, religion as the life-blood of counter-revolution. They decided to 'dechristianize' their districts, and by November this fashion reached Paris. As a new 'revolutionary calendar' replaced the old Christian one, large numbers of churches began to be closed. The aim was to stamp out all forms of Christian practice if not belief. The government, now largely vested in the hands of the Convention's Committee of Public Safety, never officially sponsored a policy which it recognized as likely to alienate more citizens than it won over, but before it was strong enough to stem the dechristianizing tide in the spring of 1794, virtually every church in France had been closed down, and throughout much of this 'Year II of Liberty' most priests were in exile or hiding.

Terror appeared to have achieved its purpose of crushing internal opposition from every quarter. Even the sansculottes, drafted into the service of a ruthless and decisive state, seemed satisfied. The fortunes of war were improving too. The *levée en masse*, an attempt to mobilize the Nation's entire human resources, proclaimed in August 1793, was helping to man and equip armies of unprecedented size. Late in December the British were driven from Toulon, and by the spring the Republic's territory was once more free from foreign occupation. By now some deputies were arguing for an end to terror. When popular leaders in Paris, called Hébertistes after their journalist spokesman Hébert, attempted to silence terror's critics by mounting a *coup d'état*, they were outmanoeuvred by the Committee of Public Safety and themselves guillotined. But Robespierre, increasingly the dominant voice on the committee, was also suspicious of the self-serving motives of the so-called 'indulgents', all friends of the unpredictable Danton, and three weeks later (5 April 1794) it was their turn to be executed. The rhythm of terror began to accelerate again, and with all political trials now channelled through the Paris revolutionary tribunal, the 2000 victims condemned there down to July made more impact on the world outside than the thousands more who had perished in previous months in the provinces. In early June the last judicial safeguards for innocence

Portrait de marie Antoinette reine de france conduite
au Supplice; dessiné à la plume par David Spectateur
du Convoi, &placé sur la fenetre avec la Citoyenne jullien
epousé du representant jullien, à qui je tiens cette piece.

8. 16 October 1793: Jacques-Louis David's sketch of Marie-Antoinette on her way to the scaffold.

were removed by the notorious Law of 22 prairial, two days after the introduction under Robespierre's sponsorship of a new, non-Christian state religion, the cult of the Supreme Being.

This was the period of the so-called 'Great Terror', often known, too, from the moralistic rationale given to it in the speeches of Robespierre, as the Republic of Virtue. Political crimes were now so widely defined that nobody felt safe. Many were now being executed almost for their counter-revolutionary potential alone: the number of noble victims, for instance, hitherto quite modest, rose markedly. What nobody could imagine was how it would all end, since even to express doubt about the need for terror was to invite suspicion. And yet the necessity for government by bloodletting was less and less obvious. The whole country was now firmly back under the Convention's control, and the armies were taking the war once more to the enemy. People began to blame the continuing terror on the suspicious mind of Robespierre, and a group of deputies who feared they might be his next target began to plot against him. Matters came to a head in a confrontation in the Convention on 26 July, when the 'Incorruptible' underwent the novel experience of being shouted down. He appealed for support the next day to the Jacobin club and to the sansculottes; but not enough rallied to him to make his appeal seem more than defiance of the Convention. He was outlawed, which meant that when he was arrested there was no need for a trial. Having failed to kill himself prior to arrest, he and his closest associates were guillotined on 28 July.

## The thermidorean dilemma

The fall of Robespierre, on 9 thermidor in the revolutionary calendar, has often been seen as the end of the Revolution. It was nothing of the sort. The terror, which did come to an end with his execution, was certainly a spectacular climax to developments since 1789, but it solved none of the problems which had torn the Revolution apart – religion, monarchy, and war. In fact it added another, in the form of Jacobinism.

Outside France, the term had become as early as 1790 shorthand for all the Revolution's excesses. Now it began to acquire the same connotations in France – a legacy of clubs, populism, social levelling, and authoritarianism in the name of these principles, all underpinned by terror. The so-called Thermidoreans in the Convention who had taken over power were committed to dismantling all that had made Jacobinism possible. Thus the prisons were emptied of suspects, the Jacobin club and its affiliates closed, economic controls like the maximum abandoned. The *assignats*, whose value had been eroded by massive overissue after war broke out, had been somewhat sustained as legal tender by the controlled economy of the Year II: now they went into free fall. As in 1788–9 accidents of nature exacerbated the situation. A mediocre harvest and perhaps the coldest winter since 1709 left the sansculottes so miserable that by the spring they were clamouring for a return to the times when bread and blood were both plentiful. In April and May (germinal and prairial in the revolutionary calendar) the Convention was twice mobbed by angry crowds and a deputy was lynched. But they lacked the old organization, and for the first time since 1789 the authorities felt they could rely on soldiers to restore domestic order. The Convention spurned the insurgents' demands; and although latter-day Jacobins would continue to dream of a return to the Year II, the people of Paris were finished as a political force for two generations. Hitherto persecuted Catholics and Royalists now began to take their revenge. In Paris, extravagantly clad 'gilded youths' beat up veteran sansculottes and Jacobin activists, while in the south a far-reaching 'White Terror' brought informal but brutal retribution to those who had wielded local power during the Year II.

If the recent past had been a series of terrible mistakes, when had they begun? Probably, thought the Thermidoreans, in 1791. Their dream was to recover the lost consensus and civic idealism of the early revolution. That meant conciliating those alienated in the meantime – Catholics and Royalists. And so although the Republic now disclaimed any religion, churches were allowed to reopen, and the policy of depopulation applied in the Vendée over the Year II was ostentatiously abandoned. Serious talk was also heard in the spring of 1795 of restoring monarchy in the person of Louis XVI's surviving son, a sickly child who might be made acceptable by a carefully controlled, public-spirited education. These hopes, however, were destroyed in June 1795 when 'Louis XVII' died; and from his exile in Verona the next month, his uncle the Count de Provence proclaimed his own succession as Louis XVIII in a chillingly uncompromising declaration which promised an almost total restoration of the old regime in the event of his return. That obviously meant giving back national lands to the Church and to émigrés who had incurred confiscation once war broke out. Some émigrés chose this moment to demonstrate their continued intransigence by attempting to invade Brittany with British support in the hope of marching on Paris at the head of a horde of Breton Royalists. They never got beyond the beaches at Quiberon and were shot in their hundreds by their republican captors.

All this blighted any hopes of a restoration. Yet, conscious that the Convention had been elected to give France a new constitution, the deputies knew they had now sat long enough. Technically, a constitution already existed: an extremely democratic one, embodying various provisions for social welfare and even the right to legalized insurrection, had been framed and adopted in 1793 in the aftermath of the downfall of the Girondins. It had been suspended at once for the war's duration. The insurgents of germinal and prairial had called for it to be implemented, but that alone ensured that it was unthinkable. Accordingly the Convention spent the summer of 1795 elaborating a new republican constitution, more heavily dependent on large property owners even than that of 1791. It was full of elaborate checks and balances, including annual elections and a constantly rotating five-man executive, the Directory. Nor did its drafters make what they saw as the fundamental mistake of 1791 by excluding themselves from the new machinery. Indeed, they insisted that two-thirds of the first deputies in the two new legislative 'councils' should be drawn from their own ranks. Royalists, who had hoped that they might win free elections, were outraged, but a mass protest in Paris was dispersed by the army under the command of young general Bonaparte (insurrection of vendémiaire: 5 October).

## The Directory

During all this time, French armies had been triumphant everywhere. Belgium was overrun, and annexed under the doctrine first proclaimed in 1793, of France's 'natural' frontiers along the Rhine. The Dutch Republic was invaded, and surrendered. The Prussians and the Spaniards made peace. By the end of 1795 only the Austrians and the British were still at war with the Republic, and neither of them threatened its territory. For 1796 a knockout blow was planned against the Emperor, with armies striking towards Vienna from Germany and Italy. The Italian command was given to Bonaparte. The front was supposed to be secondary, but in the twelve months from April 1796 he drove the Austrians out of Italy to within striking distance of their capital, and on his own initiative concluded peace preliminaries at Leoben.

Even the British were now negotiating; but the results of the first regular elections under the constitution of 1795 led all parties to drag their feet. The Directory had begun, in the aftermath of the vendémiaire insurrection, in a militant mood, and concessions were made to Jacobins persecuted since germinal and prairial. But they emerged radicalized from prison and hiding, and by the spring of 1796 some were calling for the 1793 constitution and the equalization of property. Forced underground again, a small group led by the journalist Babeuf plotted a coup. This 'conspiracy of equals', the first attempt at communistic revolution in history, was soon thwarted; but it provoked a new swing to the right which was reflected in the results of the 1797 elections. In a reaction against the remaining 'perpetuals' of the Convention, conservative and Royalist deputies were much reinforced, giving the

British and Austrians hopes of a more advantageous peace than their military position warranted. Fearing that the fruits of his Italian victories might be jeopardized, Bonaparte gave his support to three of the directors equally alarmed by the reactionary tide. In the coup of fructidor Year V (September 1797), election results were annulled in over half the departments, and 177 deputies were purged. Both subsequent rounds of election under the directorial constitution, in 1798 and 1799, would also be adjusted in accordance with political convenience; so that this constitution was never allowed the time and opportunity to work freely. There is little wonder that so few in 1799 would mourn its passing.

Meanwhile fructidor seemed to justify itself by results. The very next month the Austrians made peace at Campo Formio, recognizing the loss of Belgium and their old Italian possessions, now transformed by Bonaparte into the Cisalpine Republic, a French puppet state. At home, a confident new Directory broke the Revolution's longest-standing commitment by renouncing most of the state's debts. It acted too with renewed harshness against priests and nobles. The British, however, so far from following their Austrian allies in coming to terms, now chose to fight on alone, emphasizing their naval power in October 1797 in the victory of Camperdown. Bonaparte, back from Italy, was put in charge of invasion plans; but soon decided that the commercial British were more likely to make peace if France could threaten the source of their wealth in India. This at any rate was the main justification for his expedition to Egypt in May 1798 – although the directors were happy enough to see such an ambitious general go. The diplomatic effect, however, especially after Nelson cut him off in Egypt by destroying his fleet at the battle of the Nile in August, was to trigger the formation of a new coalition led by Russia. When Austria allowed Russian troops to cross her territory to reach the French adversary in Italy, the whole peninsula rose up against the puppet regimes set up there by Bonaparte and his successors. The French withdrew, taking the pope with them as a prisoner, and he died in French captivity. Suddenly the Republic seemed as dangerously isolated as in 1793. Was the answer the same as it had been then? Amid talk of forced loans and hostage-taking, General Jourdan moved a comprehensive law on conscription. The effect was to stir up the west once more, and produce a new Vendée in the form of a priest-led peasant uprising in the annexed Belgian territories (October 1798). It was soon put down, but the military crisis lasted until new victories the next summer, and prolonged political uncertainties as neo-Jacobins opened clubs and clamoured for emergency measures to save the country. Sieyès, re-emerging as a director after years of prudent obscurity, concluded that the constitution was unworkable. What France needed was 'authority from above, confidence from below'. He cast about for a reliable general to help him mount a coup. It was at this moment that Napoleon Bonaparte made his famous escape from the isolation of Egypt.

## Napoleon

He was more than willing to cooperate with Sieyès in dissolving the legislative councils in brumaire Year VIII (November 1799), but he, rather than his would-be patron had the decisive voice in framing the new authoritarian constitution which was promulgated after a hasty referendum in December. It invested Napoleon with practically limitless powers as First Consul of the Republic. 'Citizens', he proclaimed, 'the Revolution is established on the principles with which it began. It is over.'

None of this was true, but over the next two years Napoleon ensured that the second sentence at least began to seem credible. By defeating the Austrians (himself at Marengo in 1800, and through General Moreau at Hohenlinden the next year) he ended the war on the continent. The war-weary British gave up the struggle too in 1802 at the peace of Amiens. The revolutionary war was won, in a complete victory for France. That in turn gave Napoleon the strength to dash all Louis XVIII's hopes that he might prove the instrument of a Bourbon restoration. If

France was to have a monarch, Napoleon himself was now a more credible candidate, as he was to demonstrate by crowning himself in 1804. By then, too, he had deprived the Bourbons of their main source of support by settling the quarrel between France and Rome. Under the concordat negotiated with a new pope, Pius VII, in 1801, open Catholic worship was restored in France and paid for by the state. But to secure this deal, the pope was forced to recognize Napoleon's one precondition: that the lands of the Church confiscated and sold since 1789 were gone for ever. Their new owners could at last feel secure in their gains, and became natural supporters of the new regime, rather than of the only parties hitherto to promise them such guarantees – the discredited Directory, and the bloodstained Jacobins. The Brumaire coup itself had been glorified as saving the country from these two tainted prescriptions, and shortly afterwards the last Jacobin activists were rounded up and blamed when desperate Royalists tried to assassinate the First Consul. The nationwide sigh of relief was practically audible. Napoleonic rule would bring its own problems and contradictions, but it endured because it began by resolving others that had torn the country apart for more than a decade.

# Chapter 4
# **What it ended**

The initial impulse of the French Revolution was destructive. The revolutionaries wanted to abolish what, by the end of 1789, everybody was calling the old or former order, the ancien régime. When, in the summer of 1791, the Constituent Assembly finalized the constitution on which it had been working since June 1789, the deputies thought it would be useful in such a fundamental document to list the main things that their revolution had got rid of, what they called 'the institutions which wounded liberty and equality of rights'. And so the constitution declared that:

> There is no longer either a nobility or a peerage, or hereditary distinctions, or distinctions of orders, or a feudal regime, or any of the corporations or decorations for which proofs of nobility were required, or which implied distinctions of birth, or any other superiority but that of public officials in the exercise of their duties.
>
> There is no longer venality or heredity of public office.
>
> There is no longer for any part of the nation or for any individual any privilege or exception to the common law of all the French.
>
> There are no longer either guilds, or corporations of professions, arts and crafts.

The law no longer recognizes either religious vows or any other engagement contrary to natural rights and the constitution.

The list was far from exhaustive. In the constitution, it came immediately after the Declaration of the Rights of Man and the Citizen, which by proclaiming a number of principles of political and civil life, implicitly condemned practices opposed to them in previous times. The extended declaration which prefaced the never-implemented constitution of 1793 made this even more clear: 'The necessity of declaring these rights presupposes the presence or the recent memory of despotism.' As the Revolution proceeded, the range of its destructive ambitions widened. By 1793 they were so comprehensive that an outraged priest coined a new word to describe them: *vandalism*, evoking the anti-Christian depredations of ancient barbarians. On the other hand, the Revolution's destructive achievements often fell far short of its ambitions; and what the men of 1789 or 1793 thought they had abolished forever often reappeared, and quite soon, in forms ostensibly different but which those who had survived had no difficulty in recognizing with dismay.

## Despotism

The Revolution began as an attack on despotism. Montesquieu had defined it in *De l'Esprit des lois* (1748) as the rule of one, according to no law. Obeying no law, despotic authority was arbitrary, and its animating spirit was fear. As usual, regular usage soon diluted the original rigour of the word's meaning. Already by 1762, Rousseau was implying in his *Social Contract* that there was no meaningful difference between the authority of a despot and that of a monarch. By the end of that decade despotism was widely understood as the abuse of monarchical power, and indeed of any sort of authority. By 1789 this had come to mean above all imposing taxation without consent, arbitrary powers of arrest and imprisonment, stifling freedom of expression and opinion, and the activities of all who served these purposes, such as ministers and intendants. In a word, no distinction was now drawn between despotism, tyranny, and absolute monarchy.

The Revolution provided an opportunity to dispense with it all. By locating sovereign power in the Nation, it made the king France's servant, not its master. By subjecting him and all other officials to a constitution, it sought to replace the rule of arbitrariness by the rule of law. There was of course plenty of law under the old regime – too much, the revolutionaries thought. They saw one of their longer-term tasks as its simplification and codification. But the king had appeared able to override any of it with impunity. That was why the Bastille was such a powerful symbol – it was where unnamed state prisoners could be confined without trial, under the notorious *lettres de cachet*, sealed warrants signed by the king and revocable only by him. Once demolished, the Bastille was never rebuilt, and all that remains where it once stood is the outline of its plan in the cobblestones. Almost as powerfully symbolic was the abandonment of Versailles on 6 October 1789, the great palace which Louis XIV had made the seat of absolute monarchy. It was too big to demolish (though not to vandalize) but not even Napoleon, whose real power dwarfed that wielded by Louis XVI, thought it wise to move in there when he became a crowned ruler with a court. It evoked too many undesirable memories. Nor did Louis XVI's brothers return there after the Bourbons were restored in 1815. Even they recognized that the old nerve-centre of absolute monarchy was an inappropriate residence for constitutional rulers. Louis-Philippe, who followed them, saw that its only possible use now was as a museum.

## Aristocracy

But Versailles was more than a symbol of political authority. With its glittering population of titled courtiers, it also symbolized a whole social system dominated by a privileged nobility. From the autumn of 1788, the Revolution acquired a social thrust, and that thrust was anti-noble.

By the middle of 1789, *aristocracy* was the term used to encapsulate all that the Revolution was against. It was the quarrel over the form of the Estates-General which brought these preoccupations to the surface, and the loud and prolonged resistance of most nobles to giving up the guaranteed share of future political power that the 'forms of 1614' held out to them. Insults and exaggerations exchanged then could not be expunged; and despite the constructive role played by many noble deputies once the orders were merged, the emigration of others, and the gratuitously obstructionist behaviour of some who remained, ensured that suspicions about the nobility never died away. In June 1790 nobility itself, and the display of its appurtenances like titles and coats of arms, were forbidden by law, which only increased the sense among most nobles that they were aliens in the land of their birth. After fructidor in 1797, in the reaction against the renewed threat of royalism, nobles were indeed legally made aliens, and deprived of their rights as French citizens. They were now *ci-devants*, relics of a former time, no better than the thousands of their traitrous relatives who had emigrated rather than live in a country so changed.

Once war began, émigrés who refused to return, and for a time even those related to them, were deprived of their property. It was added to the saleable stock of national lands. But noble property was under attack almost from the beginning, in the form of the 'feudal regime' abolished on the night of 4 August 1789. Feudal rights were not always very lucrative, and their incidence varied enormously. But there was no doubt of their vast symbolic significance, as earlier peasant attacks on weather vanes and other lordly appurtenances bear witness. And although, recognized by the Assembly as a form of property, dues were supposed to go on being levied until bought out, most peasants stopped paying them at once and never offered compensation. In 1793, the Convention confirmed the *fait accompli*, and the 'time of the lords' rapidly became a mere folk memory. But the abolition of the feudal regime was only the most direct blow suffered by nobles as a result of the night of 4 August. What began as an attempt to pacify the peasantry soon broadened out into an attack on privileges in general. Nobles were already resigned to the loss of their separate fiscal status, and to a regime of careers open to talents rather than to birth or inheritance. These had been the overwhelming demand of the third estate *cahiers*, and many noble ones had also endorsed them. Now they passed into law. More subtle was the impact of the abolition of venality of offices. The ostensible point was to open the judiciary to talent and ability; but venality had been the source of many of the privileges that had proliferated since the sixteenth century, and through the sale of ennobling offices it had become the main avenue of entry into the nobility. The whole character of the French nobility had been transformed by these procedures; but now it simply ceased to recruit – a recipe for eventual extinction.

## Corporatism and privilege

But the bonfire of privileges on 4 August was general. As the implementing decree of 11 August put it: 'All particular privileges of provinces, principalities, countries, cantons, towns and communities of inhabitants, whether pecuniary or of any other nature, are irrevocably abolished, and will remain absorbed into the common law of all French people.' This was to consign the whole chaotic and luxuriant variety of the old regime to oblivion and open the way to a more rational and uniform organization of the country and of society. The old order had been corporative, every organization defining itself by its privileges and monopolies. But the revolutionaries of 1789 did not believe in monopolies of any sort, which they saw as conspiracies against the public or national interest. This included all types of professional organizations and trade guilds, which were abolished by the Allarde Law of 23 April 1791; and combinations of artisans, primitive trade unions, forbidden by the Le Chapelier law of 14 June following, which declared 'the annihilation of all sorts of corporations of citizens of the same calling or profession' to be 'one of the fundamental bases of the French constitution'.

The greatest corporation of all was of course the Church: independently wealthy, largely self-governing, and owing part of its allegiance to a foreign potentate beyond the Alps. As with the nobility, the clergy's loss of separate representation in the Estates-General heralded far more substantial damage. Clerical electors had hoped that the new regime would strengthen the role of the Catholic Church in national life after two generations of philosophic erosion, but instead the clergy found themselves appalled and apprehensive at the uncompensated abolition of tithe on 4 August. Religious freedom, vouchsafed a few weeks later in the Declaration of the Rights of Man and the Citizen, was a further blow to their spiritual monopoly. The confiscation of Church lands in November spelled the final end of the Church's independence; and made inevitable too the dissolution of monasteries and the abrogation of monastic vows in the following spring. The elective civil constitution of the clergy then destroyed the hierarchical autonomy of the Church, and priestly protests that one way or another it must give its consent to any such changes only aroused the anti-corporative fury of the National Assembly.

## The confessional state

It was not surprising that the pope anathematized the civil constitution, and his enmity was only confirmed in September 1791 when France annexed his territories of Avignon and the Comtat-Venaissin. All this meant that, when France went to war the next year, French soldiers would make a particular point of attacking ecclesiastical institutions and installations wherever they went. By the Year II the Republic had even abandoned the 'constitutional' church created under the Constituent Assembly, and had become the enemy of all religious establishment. In September 1794, although the extremes of dechristianization were over, the Republic renounced all religious affiliations; but throughout the Directory there were periodic crackdowns on suspect refractory clergy, when hundreds were sent to the 'dry guillotine' of Guiana in South America, while in Germany and

Italy territories ruled by the Church were secularized. The young Napoleon, still making his reputation, was too cautious to do more than bully the pope. But generals who succeeded him in 1798 dissolved the papal states, set up a secular 'Roman Republic', and carried the pontiff off to captivity in France. Many thought that when Pius VI died there in August 1799 the papacy itself had come to an end.

## Dynastic diplomacy

It was saved by the Austrians, who allowed a conclave to meet in Venice several months later. They did it mainly to spite the French enemy which had plagued them since 1792. In diplomatic terms the wars of the French Revolution brought to an end an uneasy and unpopular alliance with Austria which went back to 1755 and was blamed both for the disasters of the Seven Years War and for bringing Marie-Antoinette to France. But even before the break with Austria, the revolutionaries had begun to spurn the old dynastic diplomacy. When in May 1790 the King of Spain called upon France, in the name of the long-standing 'Family Compact' between the Bourbon rulers of the two kingdoms, to back Spain against Great Britain in a territorial dispute over Nootka Sound (on the Pacific coast of North America), the National Assembly refused. The new France, it declared, would only fight to preserve its national territory from attack and not to honour the private compacts of dynasts. 'It is not', one deputy later declared, 'the treaties of princes which govern the rights of nations.' This seemed to turn into something like principle the diplomatic nullity that France had fallen into in 1787, and which the decay of her army in the meantime had only compounded. That decay proved irreversible, as early defeats in the war of 1792 showed; and even if it was the trained artillery of the old regime which saved the new republic at Valmy, by the beginning of 1793 it was obvious that an entirely new sort of army would be required to fight the war of national survival that the conflict so thoughtlessly launched the previous April had become. The new army, capitalizing on the advantage of France's vast population, would be made up largely of citizen conscripts. No longer would its recruitment depend on the volunteering of drifters, its numbers sustained by regiments of foreign mercenaries. Nor would its tactics and behaviour be the self-contained, tightly controlled manoeuvres of old regime forces, dependent on their baggage trains and more concerned to preserve their own expensive existence than to take battle to the enemy. The restraint and timidity of old regime warfare can easily be caricatured and exaggerated; nevertheless it was mild indeed compared with the all-out conflict waged by the French – and, increasingly, their adversaries – over the next generation. So dynastic diplomacy, and the style of warfare which had underpinned it, scarcely survived the 1790s. When Napoleon, who built a career on mastery of the new way of fighting, attempted to buttress his monarchical pretensions by marrying an Austrian princess in 1810, it took only three years before he found himself once more at war with his father-in-law in Vienna.

## Colonial slavery

It was of course the costs of war that had brought down the old monarchy, but the crucial element in the escalation of those costs had not been the army. What had been really ruinous was the added burden of naval competition with Great Britain, where the stakes were not dynastic advantage, but worldwide economic hegemony. French hopes here had been blighted by the defeats of the Seven Years War, but not destroyed. And even if helping the Americans to their independence had not yielded the hoped-for benefits, fortunes in the Indian Ocean revived, French islands were the most flourishing in the Caribbean, and the ports serving them, such as Bordeaux and Nantes, were the most spectacularly expanding cities in the kingdom. The Revolution ruined all this for ever. A movement proclaiming equality and freedom provoked turmoil in islands built on slavery and racial discrimination. In Saint-Domingue, the most valuable territory on earth in 1789, chaos among whites and mixed-race creoles opened the way three years later to a massive uprising among the 450,000 black slaves – the greatest slave revolt in history, and the most successful. Attempts to re-establish control in 1793 culminated in the first abolition of slavery in modern times, endorsed by the Convention in Paris in February 1794. But by then renewed war against Great Britain had severed links with overseas colonies. Attempts by Napoleon during the peace of Amiens in 1802 to reimpose slavery by a military expedition to Saint-Domingue also failed, and in its aftermath the former slaves established the independent state of Haiti. Meanwhile the French slave trade had collapsed, and the economy of the great Atlantic ports shrivelled. The population of Bordeaux shrank by 15 per cent between 1790 and 1801, and seven years later Napoleon was shocked by the emptiness of its immense quayside. By then, the main impediment to maritime trade was the British navy, which had completely destroyed its French rival between 1798 and 1805, and used its triumph to impose the tightest blockade ever known on the continental coastline. But when the wars finally ended, there was no hope of ever reconstructing the old Atlantic economy of slaves, sugar, and coffee. When, a generation later, French imperial ambitions revived, Africa and Indochina would be the main targets, and commercial incentives, which had driven the creation of the pre-revolutionary empire, were secondary.

## Redrawn maps

And by then not only the French empire had fallen apart. As early as 1795 French armies destroyed the Dutch Republic and, by forcing its successor 'Batavian' sister-republic into an alliance against the British, opened Dutch colonies in three continents to the hostile depredations of the tyrant of the seas. Meanwhile the oldest political entity in Europe, the thousand-year-old Holy Roman Empire of the German Nation, was steadily dismembered, a process accelerated by Napoleon and brought to a conclusion in 1806 when he forced Francis II to resign the imperial crown and retreat into a purely Austrian hereditary monarchy. Nobody ever thought seriously of trying to revive the corpse when Napoleon fell nine years later. When, finally, Napoleon deposed the Spanish Bourbons in 1808 and flooded Spain with French troops, the world's largest and furthest-flung colonial empire absolved itself from any obligation to obey orders from Madrid. Some parts, such as Venezuela, declared their independence almost immediately. Bolívar, the 'Liberator' who led this movement, had once idolized Napoleon as a republican hero and saw the establishment of the French empire as a betrayal of revolutionary ideals. But in any case attempts by the reactionary Ferdinand VII to reimpose the old regime after the Bourbon restoration in Spain merely provoked the whole of Spanish South America into republican resistance. It had triumphed everywhere by the mid-1820s, the last ripples of the republicanism launched in Paris in 1792.

## Achievable dreams

For those who lived through all, or even part, of these vast upheavals, the shock was overwhelming. From June 1789 onwards, the diaries and observations of contemporaries echo with wonder and increasing horror at the scale of what was occurring. Nobody was prepared for it. And although from the start revolutionaries were happy to depict their movement as the triumph of eighteenth-century 'philosophy' and Enlightenment (an analysis ruefully accepted by most of their critics and enemies), it is hard to imagine either Voltaire or Rousseau revelling in the events which, from only eleven years after their deaths, were often so glibly attributed to their influence. Robespierre, as proud a disciple as any of the Enlightenment, declared: 'Political writers . . . had in no way foreseen this Revolution.' They had expected that reform, if it came at all, would occur gradually and piecemeal, and would be the work of enlightened authoritarians rather than elected representatives. In these circumstances, the sort of headlong, comprehensive change undertaken by the revolutionaries was exhilarating. The English poet Wordsworth was far from the only person to feel it a blissful moment to be alive, and that change was possible:

Not in Utopia, subterranean fields
Or some secreted island, Heaven knows where!
But in the very world, which is the world
Of all of us . . .

Nothing, in other words, needed to be accepted any more as set in
the nature of things. If the mighty French monarchy, the nobility and
the feudal law from which it justified its pre-eminence, not to
mention the Catholic Church itself, could be challenged and rejected
on grounds of rationality, utility, and humanity, then nothing was
beyond challenge. Dreams of all sorts were achievable. Rousseau had
taught that human society was hopelessly corrupt and corrupting,
and that only total change could redeem it. That was why he was
such a hero to the revolutionaries: they had proved his vision to be
possible. Never again would institutions, habits, or beliefs be
accepted merely because this was how they had always been or were
(another way of putting it) ordained by God. The Revolution
overturned for ever an innocent world of unquestioning compliance
where most things seemed beyond change or remedy. The German
philosopher Kant, in a famous essay of 1784, had defined
Enlightenment as mankind's emancipation from self-imposed
immaturity, and unwillingness to think freely for oneself. The
proposition was purely intellectual. Kant thought Enlightenment
could only progress slowly, and that a revolution would never
produce a true reform in ways of thinking. Five years later, he
changed his mind. Although he believed that no revolution was ever
justified, he convinced himself that what had happened in France was
a voluntary surrender of power by Louis XVI, because he recognized
that the moment of emancipation from unthinking routines and
supine reflexes had suddenly arrived.

# Resistance and persistence

And yet: although the Revolution symbolized the assertion of political will against the constraints of history, circumstance, and vested interest, revolutionaries soon found themselves learning the hard lesson that will alone was not enough to destroy the old regime. It fought back; and it is the strength and determination of resistance and counter-revolution that largely explains the ferocity of the terror. And when all the strength that the revolutionaries could muster had been spent, terror abandoned, and Napoleon finally defeated, many of the things that revolutionaries had sought to destroy in and after 1789 were still there, or had rapidly re-emerged. Napoleon himself, whose career is inconceivable without the Revolution, was responsible for many of the revivals. He in turn saw them as the mere recognition of political realities.

Despite dechristianization, religious practice had not been stamped out. In fact, it was the mainspring of opposition to the new order, and showed no sign of abating. The concordat with the pope, however, reconciled Catholics with the new regime by re-establishing their Church. Similarly with nobility. Born a noble himself, Napoleon knew as well as anyone that blue blood could not be abolished short of exterminating all those who believed they possessed it. And so he encouraged émigrés to return, and ignored directorial legislation depriving *ci-devants* of their citizenship. He also knew that the orders and distinctions particularly associated with nobility were the sort of 'baubles by which men are governed'. That was why he introduced the Legion of Honour, with its scarlet ribbons and insignia, in 1802. Finally, in 1808, he set up a full-blown imperial nobility, making special efforts to recruit authentic nobles from the old order to it. By then, of course, he had made himself a hereditary monarch, and he believed that no crowned head could look authentic without a court and a nobility. And his rule was even more absolute than that of the Bourbons, with prefects even more omnicompetent than those hated agents of the old 'despotism', the intendants.

When he fell, moreover, none of this disappeared. Although the line of hereditary succession would twice be interrupted, with the exception of the years 1848–52 France would be a monarchy down to 1870, under either Bourbons or a Bonaparte. Noble status would be officially recognized throughout that time, and in the 1820s émigrés would be compensated by the state for the lands they had lost in the Revolution. Prefects continued to represent authority in the country at large, and even a form of venality of offices re-emerged among notaries and other legal functionaries. The Catholic Church, meanwhile, remained established in its Napoleonic form, its priests paid out of state funds, until 1905. In 1825, Charles X, last surviving brother of Louis XVI, even underwent an elaborate coronation, in the traditional setting of Reims Cathedral, to reconsecrate the bond between his dynasty and God. A casual observer might be forgiven for concluding that all the destructive zeal of the Revolution had achieved nothing.

## Illusory restorations

But nothing would be more superficial. Apart from its gaudy trappings, the monarchy of Napoleon had little in common with that of Louis XVI. Consciously imperial, it sought to evoke Charlemagne rather than the Bourbons. There were no built-in vehicles of opposition such as the parlements or provincial estates. The nobility which the Emperor created to decorate his monarchical pretensions was much smaller than its pre-revolutionary namesake, enjoyed no legal privileges, and titles were not even hereditary without a certain level of wealth. Entry was by imperial nomination, not by purchase of venal office. More old nobles shunned the chance of joining such a factitious creation than succumbed to Napoleon's inducements.

Nor was the restored monarchy of Louis XVIII and Charles X at all like that of their martyred brother. In many respects, as has often been said, it was not his throne but Napoleon's that they inherited. None of the old regime governmental apparatus was brought back and the Civil Code remained the backbone of French law. For much of the restoration period the state was compelled to rely on men who had established themselves under the Emperor. And if the old nobility was formally recognized once again, imperial titles were still accepted and the Legion of Honour maintained. On the other hand, the Charter proclaimed by Louis XVIII in 1814, which served as the basis of a constitution down to 1848, was imbued with the spirit of 1789. In practice the restoration monarchy was constitutional, with regular elections to the lower house of a two-chamber legislature, guarantees of individual and press freedom, and equality before the law and in taxation. Above all, perhaps, the Charter, just like Napoleon when his rule began, explicitly confirmed the revolutionary land settlement. Lands confiscated from the Church and the émigrés and then sold on would not be returned to their original owners. Indeed, by granting the indemnity of 1825 to those who had lost lands, the government of Charles X unwittingly endorsed the loss. And so successive regimes professing to deplore the work of the Revolution accepted and guaranteed the massive transfer of property that it had effected.

This alone was enough to ensure that the Catholic Church restored under the concordat bore little resemblance to the former Gallican church. Without lands, endowments, or titles it was dependent on the state for all its material support apart from the pious donations of the faithful. All beneficed clergy were now state nominees. The old chaotic and uneven ecclesiastical geography had gone, too, as had the Church's exemptions and fiscal privileges, and the institutional independence of regular assemblies of the clergy. Nor were monastic orders allowed to re-establish themselves – although without endowments there would in any case have been little prospect of that. Finally, religious toleration ensured that the official confessional unity of the old regime (already crumbling, to clerical outrage, by 1789) had also gone for ever.

Although it liked to depict itself as a restoration of throne and altar, the Bourbon regime that succeeded Napoleon changed little of this. The

The French Revolution

78

more extreme, or *ultra*, supporters of the Bourbons would have liked not so much to restore the pre-revolutionary Church, as to make it even stronger than it had been then. They blamed the Revolution on the undermining of religious authority under the old regime. But their only success was the passage of an unenforceable act in 1825 stipulating the death penalty for sacrilege. Meanwhile the pious behaviour of Charles X at his coronation aroused more ridicule than reverence. The cousin who succeeded him as Louis-Philippe after the Revolution of 1830 never made any claims to rule by the grace of God, but merely as the choice of the French Nation.

## A world transformed

Attempts outside France to restore what the French Revolution or its influence had smashed were similarly doomed. Here Napoleon made no contribution. His strongest claim, indeed, to be the instrument of the Revolution is perhaps the way he systematically demolished the old order in Italy, Germany, and Spain, annihilating whole states, introducing the Civil Code and the concordat. Only in Poland, wiped off the map by partitioning powers in 1795 in the face of French impotence, and perhaps indifference, did he resurrect an echo of the old order in the Duchy of Warsaw. After all this, there was no prospect that the Congress of Vienna which met to establish a post-Napoleonic Europe could restore anything like the international old regime. In fact, it redrew frontiers and reallocated sovereigns quite as confidently as he had, and did nothing to restore any ecclesiastical principalities except the pope's own in Italy. It is true that all the great powers of the 1780s had re-emerged stronger than ever; but the 'concert of Europe' by which they sought to prevent future conflicts on a Napoleonic scale was entirely new, and owed little beyond a vaguely expressed desire for 'balance' to the ruthless and opportunistic international order of the eighteenth century. Similarly, the 'Holy Alliance' touted by East European monarchs after 1815 was more redolent of the sixteenth century than the eighteenth, and was formed to pre-empt the disruption of Europe by the forces of any other Godless revolution.

Even, therefore, when attempts were made to bring back the old regime or elements of it, these attempts could never be innocent. They were always infused, not only by awareness that it had once fallen, but also by convictions about what had brought it down, and by what might have prevented the disaster. There would be no point in restoring an old regime that was just as vulnerable as before. So no true restoration was ever possible, and although monarchies, nobilities, and churches might all reappear after revolutionary attempts to annihilate them, none of them really resembled their generic namesakes of before 1789. Despite appearances, few of the things attacked by the Revolution truly survived unscathed.

Quite literally, nothing was any longer sacred. All power, all authority, all institutions were now provisional, valid only so long as they could be justified in terms of rationality and utility. In this sense, the French Revolution really did represent the triumph of the Enlightenment, and ushered in the mental world in which we still live.

# Chapter 5
# **What it started**

The Revolution began as an assertion of national sovereignty.
Nations – not kings, not hereditary elites, not churches – were the
supreme source of authority in human affairs. It was this conviction
which led the National Assembly in 1790 to declare that France would
never make war except in self-defence, and impelled the Convention,
two years later as the new Republic appeared to have survived the
hostile onslaughts of the leagued despots of Germany, to offer
fraternity and help to all peoples seeking to recover their liberty. It
only took a few months for the Convention to recognize the
impossibility of such an open-ended pledge; and the forces unleashed
by the Revolution would be defeated, a generation later, by an alliance
of kings supported by intransigent nobles and vengeful priests who
spurned any thought that nations could be sovereign. Nevertheless a
new principle of political legitimacy had been irrevocably launched,
and within a hundred years of the apparent triumph of reaction in
1815, the sovereignty of nations had achieved acceptance throughout
Europe and the Americas. In the twentieth century it would be
invoked in its turn to expel Europeans from all their overseas
colonies.

## Totalitarian democracy

What constitutes a nation has remained problematic. Sieyès' definition of 1789, used to lambast the privileges of the nobility, was 'A body of associates living under common laws and represented by the same legislative assembly'. It proved a beginning, but no more – too loose for those who considered language, traditions, and territory at least as important. But nations, once self-defined, have seldom been content over the last two centuries to be governed by authorities not of their own choosing. The revolutionaries of 1789 assumed that national sovereignty could only be exercised representatively, but within ten years Napoleon had begun to show how it could be appropriated to legitimize dictatorship and even monarchy. Each of the steps he took between 1799 and 1804 towards making himself a hereditary emperor was endorsed by a plebiscite responding to a carefully phrased question. The results were never in doubt and all were almost certainly rigged to make them even more emphatic. His nephew Napoleon III would use the same device to give national legitimacy to his own seizure of power in 1851 and 1852; and as recently as 1958 the Fifth Republic was launched by a referendum giving vast powers to General de Gaulle. The world beyond France had to wait mostly until the twentieth century for the techniques of plebiscitary or totalitarian democracy to become widespread; but they were as firmly rooted in the great legitimizing principle of 1789 as any of the more liberal ideals also proclaimed then.

## Liberalism

The term 'liberalism' was not invented until Napoleon's power was in decline. It was first used to describe the aspirations of the Cortes of Cadiz between 1810 and 1813 to establish representative government in post-Napoleonic Spain. But what the Spanish liberals dreamed of was based on the political model first established in France by the Constituent Assembly: representative government underpinned by a written constitution guaranteeing a basic range of human rights. These would constitute the minimum demands of political reformers throughout the nineteenth century and down to the overthrow of the last absolute monarchy in Russia in 1917. The essence of liberal beliefs was to be found in the Declaration of the Rights of Man and the Citizen. That meant freedom to vote; freedom of thought, belief, and expression; and freedom from arbitrary imposition or imprisonment. Liberals believed in the equality embodied in the Declaration, which meant equality before the law, equality of rights, and equality of opportunity. They did not, however, believe in equality of property, and one of the main functions of the rule of law which they consistently invoked was to secure property owners in their absolute rights.

Beyond that there was scope for wide disagreement. Not until the twentieth century did more than a small minority accept that women should enjoy the same liberty and equality as men; and during the Revolution the few bold spirits of either sex who made liberal claims on behalf of women were ridiculed or silenced. One reason why French women had to wait so long for the political rights they finally achieved in 1944 was that the politicians of the Third Republic feared that female voters would be dominated by their priests: ever since 1793 women had proved the mainstay of Catholic resistance to revolutionary secularism. Racial equality left liberals ambivalent too. The first stirrings of anti-slavery sentiment in France coincided with the onset of the Revolution, but slaves were property, and their labours underpinned a vast network of wealth and commerce. The dangers of loosening their bonds seemed vividly demonstrated by the great slave uprising in Saint-Domingue in 1791. In an attempt to regain control there, the Convention's representatives proclaimed the abolition of slavery, and in February 1794 their action was confirmed in Paris. The deputies congratulated themselves on being the first rulers ever to abolish slavery – which they were, but only through recognizing a *fait accompli*. Napoleon in any case restored it less than ten years later in islands remaining under French control, and regimes ostensibly more liberal than his maintained it until the revolutionaries of 1848 made it part of their first business to honour the legacy of 1794.

The new Constituent Assembly that made this gesture had been elected by universal manhood suffrage – a further belated homage to a principle used to elect the Convention in 1792 but never since. Even then it had excluded servants and the unemployed. The men of 1789 had been much more restrictive. They believed that only property owners had the right to political representation: if all were now citizens, only those with a minimum level of wealth could be *active* citizens. The distinction reflected a mistrust of popular participation in public life as old as history, but which the events of the Revolution did nothing to dispel. Revolution was born amid riot, intimidation, and bloodshed in the crisis of 1789, and popular violence or the threat of it had flickered throughout the early years before bursting out with appalling carnage in the September Massacres of 1792. Everybody recognized how much the vengeful demands of the sansculottes had done to precipitate terror a year later, so that when, after it ended, the Convention produced the constitution of 1795 it deliberately set out to exclude even more people from public life than in 1791. Thereby a pattern was set for half a century, under which representative regimes would represent only the very rich, people with something to lose; and even unrepresentative regimes, like Napoleon's, would study their interests and seek to rule with their cooperation.

## The People

The problematic paradox was that a revolution which ushered in the principles of liberalism could not have come about without popular support. The people of Paris had saved the National Assembly on 14 July, and perhaps in October 1789 as well. What only counter-revolutionaries still dared to call mobs were now manifestations of the people aroused and in action, and voices could always be found to justify their excesses. The ferocious Marat, in his newspaper *The People's*

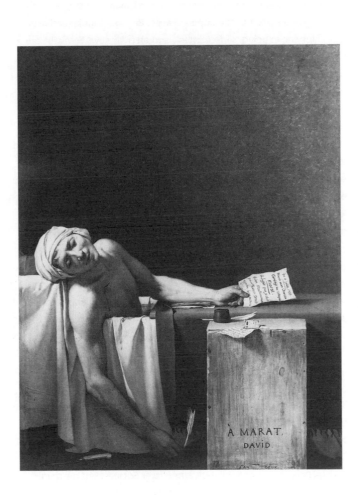

9. Marat assassinated: Jacques-Louis David's revolutionary pietà.

*Friend*, built a journalistic career on doing so, and after his assassination in 1793, was revered (and commemorated in David's most memorable painting) as a martyr to the popular cause. By 1792 popular activists were glorying in being 'sansculottes', and after the overthrow of the monarchy populist style and rhetoric dominated public life for about three years, polite forms of dress and address were abandoned, and political rights were equalized (at least among men). An egalitarian constitution was proclaimed or at any rate promised, vouchsafing free education and 'the social guarantee' of welfare support for the indigent, the sick, and the disabled. Meanwhile the rich were mulcted in a forced loan, there was talk of redistributing the property of émigrés and traitors to poor patriots, and prices of basic commodities were kept low by the maximum. All these policies were abandoned after the fall of Robespierre; but almost at once they began to be regarded by many as the lost promise of true social equality. Babeuf and his co-conspirators of 1796 proposed to base their seizure of power on the never-implemented constitution of 1793. Later, Socialists would look back to the Year II of the revolutionary calendar to find the earliest 'anticipations' of their ideals at the moment when the People entered politics for the first time in pursuit of their own interests, rather than as the tools of more powerful manipulators.

## Terror

But here too there was a problematic paradox. The Year II was also the time of the terror, whose last phase at least looked very like social revenge in action. Were popular power and terror inseparable? Drawing on theoretical justifications framed at the time by orators such as Robespierre or Saint-Just, some later Socialist or Communist revolutionaries did not shrink from accepting that only extermination would defeat the enemies of the people. There could be no true revolution without terror. And although the nineteenth century shuddered at the memory of the revolutionary tribunal and the show trials it conducted, the twentieth would see them echoed under many regimes claiming legitimacy from revolutions. Many later sympathizers with the Revolution's broad aspirations were understandably reluctant to believe that society could only be made more equal through bloodshed. They, along with liberals who were as concerned by the threats to property heard in the Year II as the threats to life, saw the terror as at best a cruel necessity, forced upon the First Republic not by the inexorable logic of the Revolution but by the force of 'circumstances'. In a country divided by rashly imposed religious choices and the feckless behaviour of Louis XVI and his queen, the fortunes of war dictated extreme measures of national defence as the distinction between opposition and treason became blurred. But the Revolution was a warning of what might happen rather than a prescription of what must.

## Left and right

All such perceptions were grounded in the conviction that, however mixed its character, there was more good in the Revolution than bad. This was the view from the left, itself a way of describing politics which originated in the Revolution, when proponents of further change tended in successive assemblies to sit on the left of the president's chair, while conservatives congregated on his right. The right, in fact modern political conservatism, was as much a creation of the French Revolution as all the things it opposed. The instinctive inertia of the ancien régime had gone forever: those who sought to preserve governments, power structures, and social institutions from revolution in the new sense were obliged to formulate unprecedented rationales and strategies for doing so.

## Conspirators and revolutionaries

The collapse of the old order, and the headlong changes that followed, took everyone by surprise. In the confusion of the next five years, with ever more horrific news of destruction, outrage, and massacre,

10. The enduring legend: Eugène Delacroix's *Liberty Leading the People* (1830).

bewildered onlookers cast about for explanations for such a boundless upheaval. Hostile observers thought it could only be a conspiracy. As a network of political clubs, the Jacobins, emerged as the vectors of the revolutionary radicalism, it began to be suspected that these were none other than the mysterious freemasons who had proliferated so spectacularly over the eighteenth century. Deistic but tolerant (and condemned twice for that by the Catholic Church) and glorying in secrecy while invoking values such as liberty, equality, and benevolence, masonic aims and ideas seemed in retrospect to be corrosive of all established values – even though the old elites had flocked to join lodges. No credible causal link has ever been established between freemasonry and the French Revolution or indeed the Jacobin clubs, but in 1797 a book purporting to demonstrate their connection in a plot to subvert religion, monarchy, and the social hierarchy was a Europe-wide bestseller. Barruel's *Memoirs to Serve for the History of Jacobinism* remained in print into the twentieth century, reflecting an undying suspicion of a movement that before 1789 had alarmed nobody except a few paranoid priests. So indelibly, indeed, did freemasonry now come to be associated in certain continental countries with republicanism and anti-clericalism, that to join a lodge became a gesture of radical political conviction – which it had never been before the Revolution. Conservative regimes, right down to the Nazis and their Vichy puppets, would accordingly continue to view freemasonry with the deepest suspicion, and would periodically close its networks down.

Nor were such suspicions entirely groundless, in the sense that throughout the nineteenth century many political radicals had come to believe that the way to bring about revolution actually was through secret conspiracies. Before 1789 there was no such thing as a revolutionary. Nobody believed that an established order could be so comprehensively overthrown. But once it was shown to be possible, the history of France in the 1790s became the classic episode of modern history, whether as inspiration or warning, a model for all sides of what to do or what to avoid. Not even sympathizers could afford to accept that conspiracy was not a way to achieve revolution, because otherwise it would be the work of a blind fate beyond the influence of conscious human agency. And so the 1790s themselves saw secret groups plotting revolution in many countries of Europe. In Poland and Ireland they played a significant part in bringing about vast and bloody uprisings. Their defeated leaders who had turned to France for help, men like Tadeusz Kosciuszko and Wolfe Tone, have been revered ever since as prophets or martyrs of national independence. And when the Revolution in France itself began to disappoint its adherents, a genuine Jacobin plot was hatched – but against the new regime rather than the old. The first attempt in history at communist revolution, Babeuf's 'conspiracy of equals' of 1796 failed miserably; but his co-conspirator Buonarroti spent the rest of a long life setting up conspiratorial revolutionary networks, and perpetuated the memory of the first one in a book of 1828 (*Conspiracy for Equality*) which inspired three generations of subversives and became a sacred text of successful Communism after the Russian Revolution of 1917. Throughout the first quarter of the twentieth century, in fact, when Russia experienced two revolutions, French precedents became an obsession among Russian intellectuals, and in 1917 even the leading players brooded constantly on who were the Jacobins, who the Girondins, and whether a Napoleon was lurking among them.

## Patterns and paradigms

In France itself, meanwhile, recourse to further revolution had been a standard, and for many people entirely reputable, political option for much of the nineteenth century. When in 1830 Charles X seemed poised to abandon even the attenuated parts of the revolutionary legacy accepted by his brother Louis XVIII as the price for succeeding Napoleon, he was overthrown by three days of insurgency on the streets of Paris. His cousin and successor Louis-Philippe ostentatiously flew the tricolour, and hoped to reconcile the bitterly divided traditions originating in 1789. He failed, and was driven out in his turn by more popular defiance in the revolution of 1848. Another Bonaparte closed this one off, but his defeat in the Franco-Prusssian War led to the bloodiest episode since the terror – the Paris Commune of 1871 in which perhaps 25,000 people died. The very name commune evoked 1792, and many *communards* saw themselves as sansculottes reincarnate, fighting the same enemies as the First Republic – Royalists, Catholics, duplicitous generals, and the greedy rich. Only the last category derived much benefit from their defeat, however, and the Third Republic which emerged from the traumas of the early 1870s would glory in revolutionary imagery and modestly pursue democratic and anti-clerical aspirations first articulated in the 1790s. For half a century after 1917, many French intellectuals regarded the Russian Revolution as the belated fulfilment of the promise of their own, and the historiography of the revolutionary decade was dominated by members of or sympathizers with the French Communist party. But their grip on the Revolution began to be challenged from the mid-1950s, and, as the Soviet empire crumbled in 1989, the hegemonic interpretation of the bicentennial year was that of the neo-conservative, ex-Communist François Furet.

Although he saw terror as inherent in the Revolution from its very beginning, Furet nevertheless saw the revolutionary experience as the foundation of modern political culture. Americans have the best grounds for disputing this, with a founding revolution that preceded the French one by more than a decade. Having helped to make American independence possible, many French contemporaries certainly found the transatlantic example inspiring, but nobody thought it could be transplanted to Europe. By the time that most enduring monument to eighteenth-century political creativity, the United States constitution, was finalized, the French were engaged in their own constitution-making and claiming, with some justice, that their revolution was like no other in history, and owed little except fraternal good feeling to previous upheavals elsewhere. The Americans themselves were soon enough bitterly divided about whether the new France was in any sense the same country which had helped them to independence, and uncertain about how much of its new regime they could admire. Remote from the older continent, ambivalent about contacts with it, and speaking what was still a peripheral language, America was marginalized by the French Revolution until the twentieth century – even if it owed its westward expansion to the sale by Napoleon of Louisiana in 1803.

## Conservatism, reaction, and religion

Convinced, meanwhile, that what had allowed an old regime of stability, deference, and order to be overthrown was a lack of vigilance, European conservatism struck out at the sources of subversion. Before the 1790s were out, all governments were rapidly expanding their repressive resources, with a proliferation of spies and informers and experiments with regular public police forces. Lists of suspects would be routinely kept and their movements tracked. Strict censorship would be imposed on all forms of publishing, and the press, blamed for disseminating insubordination and free thought both before and during the Revolution, subjected to the closest supervision. Among the most efficient of these repressive regimes would be that of Napoleon himself, who, although a product of the Revolution, sought to ground his appeal in reassuring property owners that the social threat of Jacobinism had been stifled. Napoleon also recognized that the original, and still the deepest, wound inflicted on France by the Revolution had been the quarrel with the Roman Catholic Church; and nothing did more to bring the Revolution to an end than his concordat with Pius VII. He was convinced, like all conservative regimes after him throughout the nineteenth century, that the firmest support for order and authority lay in a secure and recognized role for organized religion, in which he saw nothing more or less than 'the mystery of the social order'.

Traumatized by the experience of the 1790s, which included the first attempt in history in 1793 to stamp out religious practice entirely, and then the renunciation by the Convention the next year of all religious affiliation (the first overt creation in the history of Europe of a secular state), the Church for its part was only too eager to renew its age-old alliance with secular powers. The experience proved less than satisfactory. Within eight years of concluding the concordat, Pius VII found himself, like his predecessor, a French prisoner, deprived of his central Italian dominions, and about to undergo four years of relentless bullying by Napoleon. From imprisonment on St Helena, the former emperor claimed that he had planned to abolish the papacy outright. The Bourbons who succeeded him were much friendlier towards the Church, but they had long given up any idea of returning it to its position of before 1789. An attempt to renegotiate the concordat foundered, and the new regime confirmed the loss of Church lands which Napoleon had insisted the pope accept as a precondition of the original negotiation. From now on the fortunes of the Church echoed every vicissitude in the French state throughout a turbulent century; and when eventually that state became a republic vaunting its descent from the one which had severed all links between Church and state in 1794, the course was set for a separation which eventually occurred in 1905. Beyond France meanwhile, although the pope received his Italian territories back in 1814, ecclesiastical rule was not restored anywhere else in Europe, and Italian nationalists increasingly regarded the papal states as the main obstacle to unifying the peninsula. Until the downfall of Napoleon III in 1870, monarchical France was the papacy's main supporter; but, increasingly embattled, Pius IX fell back upon powers that were not of this world. The end of French support, and with it the absorption of former papal territories into the new kingdom of Italy, coincided with the promulgation by the Vatican Council of the doctrine of papal infallibility – never before unambiguously claimed for fear of the reactions of secular rulers. And what the experience of Church–state relations had demonstrated since 1790 was that faith was at least as likely to flourish without the backing of the state as with it. The lesson was reinforced when the new German empire launched the *Kulturkampf* against the Catholic Church in the 1870s. Rome would continue to anathematize the French Revolution as the origin of modern impiety and anti-clericalism, a change happily accepted by all those who gloried in these attitudes. But the traumas of the 1790s also began a process of slow recognition within the Church that it might be better off independent of secular authority, free to make its own decisions and demanding only toleration for its practices and activities. When power was offered it, as in mid-twentieth-century Spain, or in Ireland, the clergy still found it hard to resist; but in a world (again traceable to the French Revolution) where regular political change was normal and to be expected, the unwisdom of identifying too closely with any regime, however sympathetic, has become more and more obvious to thoughtful churchmen.

The Church continued, after all, to pay the penalty of clinging too closely to reactionary and repressive regimes throughout the nineteenth century. As late as the 1920s, the later stages of the Mexican revolution brought conscious echoes of the dechristianization of 1793, and the *Cristero* revolt of devout Indians in support of the embattled church recalled the Vendée revolt of that same year. The last great triumph of extreme anti-clericalism, however, struck not so much at the Catholic Church (or at least not until it reached Poland, Czechoslovakia, and Hungary after 1945) as the Russian Orthodox. By 1922, Lenin had 'reached the firm conclusion that we must now instigate a decisive and merciless battle against the clergy, we must suppress their opposition with so much cruelty that they will not forget it for several decades. The more . . . we succeed in shooting for this reason, the better'. Like several of the more zealous dechristianizers of 1793, Stalin had trained before the Revolution as a priest, and the Soviet Union under his rule was officially committed to atheism and the eradication of 'superstition'. Most churches were closed, many demolished, and devotion was largely kept alive (as in France in the 1790s) by peasant women. These policies were maintained, although less ruthlessly, after his death; and yet the Church re-emerged as the Soviet Union collapsed. Its East European satellite regimes, meanwhile, knew better than to confront the Catholic Church too fiercely. The emergence of a pope from Poland in 1978 might be seen, in retrospect, as a sign of the Church's recovering confidence at the moment when an ideology of extreme secularism first formulated almost two centuries earlier was beginning to crumble.

## Rationalization

The revolutionary critique of religion, even before it became an all-out attack, was part of the wider commitment of the men of 1789 to promoting rationality in human affairs. The collapse of the old regime, they thought, presented them with an opportunity to take control of their circumstances and remould them according to a conscious plan or set of principles. Nobody before had ever had such an extraordinary chance. When their armies and Napoleon's in turn overthrew other old regimes, they gave their subjects - forced upon them, indeed - the same chance. The keynote of all the new arrangements and institutions which now appeared was rationality and uniformity. Administrative maps and boundaries were redrawn, divisions equalized, anomalies of all sorts eliminated. The departments into which France was then divided remained unmodified until the twentieth century. Uniformity of means of exchange and communication was also introduced - currency, weights and measures, and language; underpinned by a centralized and carefully regulated system of education, and a simple, concise code of laws. Some of these things were only sketched out or barely begun in the 1790s; but the drive and singleness of purpose of Napoleon fixed most of them firmly in place and established them all as goals to be pursued by successive regimes. This was how modern states organized themselves. It is true that, under the inexorable pressure of interstate competition, moves in this direction had already been underway in a number of countries before 1789: but they were bitterly contentious, and it was contention over just such moves that brought down the French old regime. The Revolution swept the institutions and forces of resistance aside, both in France and wherever else French power

What it started

reached. In so doing, it offered an object lesson to all regimes of how easy modernization could be, given determination.

Or so it seemed. In reality, the victories of the French Revolution had been far from easy. They had only been secured though paranoid savagery at home and military ruthlessness abroad. To the 16,000 official victims of the terror should be added perhaps 150,000 more who perished in the fighting and reprisals of 1793-4. The devastated Vendée, in fact, has been identified by some of its most recent historians as the first modern attempt at genocide. The wars against old regime Europe between 1792 and 1815 cost the lives of well over 5 million Europeans (1.4 million of them French) – a slaughter as great, although over a longer period, as that of the war of 1914-18. Such costs were overlooked, or brushed aside, by later observers inspired by the ambitions and achievements of the revolutionaries. The corollary was that when such enthusiasts triumphed, as in twentieth-century Russia or China, the carnage was repeated. Nor have the victories achieved at such cost endured.

## A limited legacy

The legacy of the French Revolution to the nineteenth century, we have seen in this chapter, was momentous, but always partial and often paradoxical. The regimes of revolutionary Communism established in the twentieth century have not outlasted it in Europe, and those still surviving beyond are transforming themselves in ways which would have outraged their founding fathers. What has defeated the revolutionary impulse in the long term is the persistence of cultural diversity. Rationalizing ideologies imposed by state power, and the intellectuals and administrators who have placed such faith in them since 1789, have never succeeded in effacing the importance of less rational sources of identity in habits, traditions, religious beliefs, regional and local loyalties, or distinct languages. Perhaps the most ambitious of all the Revolution's rationalizations was the attempt to restart time itself from the founding of the republic in September 1792. The very months were rescheduled and renamed, and seven-day weeks replaced by ten-day 'decades'. It never caught on, and the revolutionary calendar was officially abandoned by Napoleon at the end of the year XIV (1806). It was a portent of many other failures of reason in the face of human resistance or indifference. And with the collapse since the mid-1980s of most of the world's regimes of Communist universalism, these forces have re-emerged with renewed vigour. Even in countries where Communism never triumphed in the twentieth century, including France, decentralization and devolution, acknowledgement of linguistic diversity, and abandonment by the state of obligations too readily assumed or acquired, marked the last two decades of the twentieth century. As the bicentenary of 1989 recedes, what was intended as a celebration of the enduring values launched by the Revolution begins to seem more like their funeral.

# Chapter 6
# **Where it stands**

'The whole business now seems over', wrote the English observer Arthur Young in Paris on 27 June 1789, 'and the revolution complete.' People would repeatedly make the same observation, usually more in hope than conviction, over the next ten years until Napoleon officially proclaimed the end of the Revolution in December 1799. Even then all he meant was the end of a series of spectacular events in France; he was to continue to export them for another sixteen years. Besides, the Revolution was not simply a meaningless sequence of upheavals. These conflicts were about principles and ideas which continued to clash throughout the nineteenth century, and would be reinvigorated by the triumphs of Marxist Communism in the twentieth. Thus it still seemed outrageous to many French intellectuals when, in 1978, the historian François Furet proclaimed, at the start of a celebrated essay, that 'The French Revolution is finished' (*terminée*).

## A historical challenge

What he meant was that the Revolution was now, or ought to be, a subject for historical enquiry as detached and dispassionate as that of medievalists studying (his example) the Merovingian kings. Whereas the history of the Revolution as it has been written in France for much of the twentieth century had been more a matter of commemoration than scholarly analysis, its legitimacy monopolized by a succession of

Communists or fellow-travellers entrenched in the university hierarchy. Furet's attack was suffused with personal history. Though a Sorbonne graduate, he had always despised the university world, and had built a career in the rival *Ecole pratique des Hautes Etudes* (later EHESS). A Communist in youth, like so many others he was disillusioned by the Soviet invasion of Hungary in 1956, and renounced the party. And when he and a fellow apostate, Denis Richet, wrote a new history of the Revolution in 1965, they were unanimously denounced by leading specialists in the subject as intruders, not qualified in the subject, who, in offering an interpretation suggesting that it had 'skidded off course', had traduced the Revolution's essential unity of purpose and direction. By 1978 Furet had abandoned this view, but not the enmities it had aroused. For the rest of his life (he died in 1997), he pressed home his attack, particularly during the debates of the bicentenary. As that year came to an end, he cheerfully proclaimed that he had won.

## The classic interpretation

What had he defeated? He called it the 'Jacobino-Marxist Vulgate'. His opponents called it the 'classic' interpretation of the Revolution. Its basis was (and is, since despite Furet's triumphalism it retains many adherents) the conviction that the Revolution was a force for progress. The fruit and vindication of the Enlightenment, it set out to emancipate not just the French, but humanity as a whole, from the grip of superstition, prejudice, routine, and unjustifiable social inequities by resolute and democratic political action. This was the 'Jacobin' bedrock, differing little from the professions of countless clubbists in the 1790s. As a historical interpretation, it built on the work of nineteenth-century custodians of revolutionary traditions, most famously perhaps Jules Michelet, that apocalyptic idolizer of 'The People'. Confident and complacent, the Jacobin perspective was disturbed only by the terror, which it did not seek to defend except as a cruel necessity and a reflex of national defence.

Around the turn of the twentieth century, this historiographical Jacobinism began to acquire a new political overlay. From 1898 the great left-wing politician Jean Jaurès began to produce a *Socialist History of the French Revolution* which emphasized its economic and social dimensions and introduced an element of Marxist analysis. Marx himself had written little directly on the Revolution, but it was easy enough to fit a movement which had begun with an attack on nobles and feudalism into a theory of history that emphasized class struggle and the conflict between capitalism and feudalism. The French Revolution from this viewpoint was the key moment in modern history, when the capitalist bourgeoisie overthrew the old feudal nobility. The fundamental questions about it were therefore economic and social. At the very moment when Jaurès was writing, a fierce young professional historian, Albert Mathiez, was beginning a lifelong campaign to rehabilitate Robespierre, under whose terroristic rule clear 'anticipations' of later socialist ideals had appeared. Mathiez set out to stamp his own viewpoint on the entire historiography of the Revolution, and his native vigour was redoubled from 1917 by the example and inspiration of the Bolshevik Revolution in Russia, which seemed to revive the lost promise of 1794. Robespierre's Republic of Virtue would live again in Lenin's Soviet Union. Mathiez only belonged briefly to the Communist Party, but he established a parallel historical party of his own in the form of a 'Society of Robespierrist Studies'. Its journal, the *Annales Historiques de la Révolution française*, is still the main French-language periodical devoted to the Revolution. Apart from the years of Vichy, when it was silenced, from the death of Mathiez in 1932 until the advent of Furet this society and its members dominated teaching and writing about the Revolution in France, and its successive leading figures occupied the chair of the History of the Revolution at the Sorbonne. When Furet launched his polemics, the incumbent of this apostolic succession was the lifelong Communist Albert Soboul (d.1982), against whose convictions the waters of what he naturally called 'revisionism' broke in vain.

## Revisionism

But revisionism had not begun with Furet. It originated in the English-speaking world in the 1950s – in England with Alfred Cobban, in the USA with George V. Taylor. Although many of the great minds of nineteenth-century anglophone culture had been fascinated by the French Revolution and Napoleon, interest lapsed during the first half of the twentieth century. The handful of historians still attracted to the subject worked little in France and achieved almost no recognition there. After the Second World War, however, as Western democracy appeared threatened by Marxists both domestic and foreign, it seemed urgent to rescue the great episodes of modern history from tendentious distortions. Both Cobban and Taylor chose to confront what they called the French 'orthodoxies' head-on. It was a myth, Cobban claimed, that the revolutionaries of 1789 were the spokesmen of capitalism; the deputies who destroyed the ancien régime were office-holders and landowners. In any case, Taylor argued, most pre-revolutionary wealth was non-capitalist, and such capitalism as there was had no interest in the destruction of the old order. That destruction, indeed, so far from sweeping away the obstacles holding back a thrusting capitalist bourgeoisie, proved an economic disaster and drove everyone with money to invest in the security of land. Taking their cue from the vast range of questions raised by these critiques, throughout the 1960s and 1970s a new generation of scholars from English-speaking countries invaded the French archives to test the new hypotheses. By the 1980s they had largely demolished the empirical basis and the intellectual coherence of the 'classic' interpretation of the Revolution's origins.

Initially the French maintained their traditional disdain for the 'Anglo-Saxons', dismissing Taylor and Cobban as cold warriors who had read too much Burke and wished only to disparage the Revolution as a continuing threat to the hegemony of the Western bourgeoisie. But when Furet and Richet challenged the classic interpretation from within the introverted world of French culture, the Robespierrists were forced onto the defensive. Furet, who had no problems with the English language, had by the early 1970s begun to incorporate the findings and arguments of the foreigners into his own interpretations; as well as those of a compatriot long neglected in France but always taken seriously by English speakers, Alexis de Tocqueville (d. 1859). Tocqueville saw the Revolution as the advent of democracy and equality but not of liberty. Napoleon and his nephew, whom this aristocrat of old stock hated, had shown how dictatorship could be established with democratic support, since the Revolution had swept away all the institutions which, in impeding the relentless growth of state power, had kept the spirit of liberty alive. These insights persuaded Furet that the Revolution had not after all skidded off course into terror. The potential for terror had been inherent right from the start, from the moment when national sovereignty was proclaimed and no recognition given to the legitimacy of conflicting interests within the national community. For all its libertarian rhetoric, the Revolution had no more been disposed to tolerate opposition than the old monarchy, and the origins of modern totalitarianism would be found in the years between 1789 and 1794.

## Post-revisionism

This was more than revisionism. The approach of Cobban, Taylor, and those who came after them has largely been empirical, undermining the sweeping social and economic claims of the classic interpretation with new evidence, but seldom seeking to establish new grand overviews. The most they claimed was that the Revolution could be more convincingly explained in terms of politics, contingency, and perhaps even accident. This is largely the approach adopted in earlier chapters of this book. Such suggestions did not satisfy bolder minds. As Furet began to depict a Revolution in the grip of attitudes and convictions which propelled it inevitably towards terror, others, mostly in America, sought wider explanations for revolutionary behaviour in cultural terms. They saw a number of 'discourses' emerging from the political conflict between 1770 and 1789, which laid the foundation for much of the uncompromising language and arguments of the revolutionaries. Borrowing from the speculations of the German left-wing philosopher Jürgen Habermas, they argued that in the generation before the Revolution public opinion escaped from the king's control, and that in the process respect and reverence for the monarchy ebbed away. Furet found these interpretative trends even more congenial than those of early revisionism, and spent increasing amounts of time in America and at conferences abroad, where yet another generation of young scholars committed to the cultural approach treated the triumphs of revisionism as yesterday's battles. By 1987, these trends were crystallizing into a new orthodoxy, and were being labelled as post-revisionism.

## The bicentenary

Whatever might be said against the classic interpretation, it was at least coherent and comprehensible. By contrast, the 'linguistic turn' of post-revisionism, increasingly influenced by philosophers and literary theorists, produced much abstruse material that could barely be understood outside specialist circles. When, therefore, the Socialist president of France decreed, some years in advance, that the revolutionary bicentenary of 1989 must be celebrated, he entrusted the academic side of the festivities to the still well-entrenched defenders of what Soboul had called, just before he died, 'our good old orthodoxy'. Soboul's successor at the Sorbonne, Michel Vovelle, was given a worldwide mission of coordinating academic commemoration. He worked so hard at it that eventually doctors instructed him to stop. But the learned bicentenary proved just as unmanageable as the more public one. While both Vovelle and Furet toured colloquia in every continent, they never appeared together on the same platform, and Furet and his cohorts boycotted the biggest conference of the year organized by Vovelle in Paris. This was scarcely the attitude of scholarly detachment for which Furet had seemed to be calling in 1978. As a

11. Scholarly overload: The reaction of reviewers to the bicentenary
(*Daily Telegraph*, 3 June 1989).

subject arousing sectarian passions, the Revolution was clearly far from finished, even for those claiming it was.

The bicentenary, in fact, released a torrent of vituperative publishing, most of it denouncing one aspect or another of the Revolution and its legacy. Particularly vocal in France were defenders of the Vendée rebels, the most persistent contemporary French enemies of the Revolution, and in consequence victims of the most savage repression. The heroism of devout peasant guerillas, long derided as superstitious fanatics, was now lovingly chronicled. Catholic clergy reminded their flocks of when modern impiety had begun. In the English-speaking world, meanwhile, while hundreds of learned gatherings picked over the debris of a generation of scholarly clashes, and publishers and the media felt obliged to mark the bicentenary in one way or another, the sensation of the year was the publication of Simon Schama's *Citizens*, a vast 'chronicle' of the Revolution which ignored the historical debate almost entirely in the interests of telling a colourful and lurid story. The overall message was the folly of undertaking revolutions (one fortunately lost on the East Europeans who were at that moment defying Soviet satellite regimes). Yet there was an intellectual stance behind Schama's Dickensian narrative, and it was basically the same as Furet's. The terror, declared the most famous sentence in the book, was merely 1789 with a higher body count; and 'violence . . . was not just an unfortunate side effect . . . it was the Revolution's source of collective energy. It was what made the Revolution revolutionary'. Significantly, Schama's tale ended abruptly in 1794 with the fall of Robespierre and the end of the terror.

One of the favourite mantras of the Revolution's classic interpreters was taken from Georges Clemenceau, the statesman of the Third Republic who gloried in the achievements of the First. The Revolution, he declared, was a *bloc*. It had to be accepted in its totality, terror and all. It could not be disaggregated. Revisionism, with its emphasis on the contingent, the accidental, and the reality of choices facing those involved, suggested otherwise – as had the young Furet when he and

Richet spoke of the Revolution skidding off course. Only by approaching events as contemporaries had to, without an awareness of horrors to come, could regicide, dechristianization, and the guillotine be prevented from throwing their shadows over what preceded them, as they did over everything that followed. Post-revisionists, however, turned against this approach. In emphasizing the cultural constraints that determined what history's actors could or could not think or do, they opened the way to a determinism not unlike that of the economic and social factors emphasized by the classic historians in their Marxist-inspired heyday. And in insisting that terror was inherent in the Revolution from the start, Furet made it the central issue by which to judge the movement's entire significance. For post-revisionists of all stamps, in fact, the Revolution was as much a *bloc* as it was for those they claimed to have vanquished.

It was, of course, a different sort of *bloc*. And while the post-revisionist emphasis on the centrality of terror encouraged blanket denunciations not only of the Revolution but also of the very attempt to commemorate it, there were also plenty of celebrations throughout France, as Mitterrand intended, of two hundred years of human rights. Vovelle, for his part, while reiterating his commitment to left-wing values traceable back to Jacobinism, refused to accept that there had been any sort of contest with Furet, observing meekly that scholarly enquiry was open to all viewpoints. But, apart from a few hard-line Communists, the adherents of the once-hegemonic classic tradition emerged from the bicentenary chastened. In the 1990s, the *Annales Historiques de la Révolution* began gingerly to open its pages to non-members of the Robespierrist studies circle, and to review their books for purposes other than denunciation. The chair of Mathiez, Soboul, and Vovelle is now occupied by a historian of the Vendée. And although since the death of Furet new sympathetic analyses of Jacobinism have begun to appear, they have been anxious to deny that terror was part of its mainstream. The heaviest blows, however, were not delivered by scholarly revisionists or post-revisionists. They came from the

spectacular collapse of Soviet Communism, and the repressive attempts
of its Chinese variant, just a few weeks before 14 July 1989, to shore up
its authority against students calling for liberty and singing the
*Marseillaise*.

## The end of a dream?

Awareness of the full repressive record of Soviet Communism had been
growing at least since Krushchev had begun to denounce Stalin in 1956.
But so long as the Soviet Union continued apparently flourishing and
powerful, it could be argued that its Marxist ideology worked and that
its bloody past had been a worthwhile price to pay to secure popular
democracy. Similar arguments had been used to justify terror in 1793–4,
and by later pro-Jacobin historians. When the rule of Gorbachev
revealed the whole Soviet edifice to be unviable, and incapable of
sustaining its sister-republics in Eastern Europe, this delusion collapsed.
A regime invested for seventy years with all the hopes and dreams
repeatedly frustrated since the fall of Robespierre had proved scarcely
more successful, and at far heavier human cost, than the prototype
which it and its friends held in reverence. The Chinese, whose historical
loyalties were similar, had no answer to their own domestic critics other
than to shoot or imprison them. If such regimes were the true heirs of
the French Revolution, then Tocqueville and Furet were right in their
perception that its significance lay not in the enhancement of liberty but
in the promotion of state power. Faith in the benevolent potential of a
rationalizing state was the first, and perhaps the last, illusion of the
Enlightenment; and in this sense the French Revolution, and all the
others that followed over two hundred years, were its authentic heirs.
The illusion died whilst historians in the West squabbled about how, or
even whether, to mark the Revolution's second centenary.

But of course totalitarian peoples' democracy was not the only legacy of
ways of thinking that first triumphed in the 1790s. François Mitterrand's
decision to celebrate the rights of man at the bicentenary was more

than a doomed attempt to dissociate the memory of the Revolution from the terror. It was also a recognition that the ideology of human rights was, if anything, more important than it had ever been. Regimes of tyranny and massacre have no monopoly in the heritage of the Revolution. Citizens of modern constitutional democracies whose civil and political rights are guaranteed, and whose life chances are equal before the law, can find much in it to celebrate. The ambition of the French Revolution was so comprehensive that almost anyone living since can find something there to admire as well as to deplore. Nor are all the battles it launched yet over. If the collapse of Communism can be seen as defeat for Jacobins, the European Union looks very like a Girondin project to bring the liberal benefits of 1789 to Europe as a whole. In turn, this aspiration meets most resistance from national reflexes first fully aroused by the challenges emanating from revolutionary France. 'The barest enumeration of some of the principal consequences of 1789', wrote an eminent literary critic in 1987, even before the full symbolic significance of the bicentennial year had emerged,

> enforce the realisation that the world as we know it today ... is the composite of reflexes, political assumptions and structures, rhetorical postulates, bred by the French Revolution. More than arguably, for it entails subsequent, so often mimetic revolutionary movements and struggles across the rest of the planet, the French Revolution is the pivotal historical-social date after that of the foundation of Christianity ... Time itself, the cycle of lived history, was deemed to have begun a second time ... 1789 continues to be now.
>
> G. Steiner, 'Aspects of Counter-Revolution', in G. Best (ed.)
> *The Permanent Revolution*

The last word, however, should perhaps be left to the author with whom this book began. 'That, my dear Algy', says Ernest Worthing, 'is the whole truth pure and simple.' 'The truth', his friend replies, 'is rarely pure and never simple.'

# Timeline: Important dates of the French Revolution

## BEFORE

## DURING

27 May. Orders finally unite

14 July. Bastille falls

July. 'Great Fear' in countryside

4 Aug. Abolition of feudalism, privileges, and venality

26 Aug. Declaration of Rights of Man and the Citizen

5–6 October. 'October Days': women march to Versailles, king and Assembly move to Paris

2 Nov. Church property nationalized

12 Dec. *Assignats* introduced.

1790

13 Feb. Monastic vows forbidden

22 May. Foreign conquests renounced

19 June. Nobility abolished

12 July. Civil Constitution of the Clergy

16 Aug. Parlements abolished

27 Nov. Oath of the clergy

Nov. Burke, *Reflections on the Revolution in France*

1791

Mar. Paine, *Rights of Man*

2 Mar. Guilds dissolved

13 Apr. Pope condemns Civil Constitution

14 May. Le Chapelier law bans trade unions

20–21 June. Flight to Varennes

16 July. Louis XVI reinstated

17 July. Champ de Mars massacre

14 Aug. Slave rebellion in Saint-Domingue

27 Aug. Declaration of Pillnitz

14 Sept. Louis XVI accepts constitution

30 Sept. Constituent Assembly dissolved

1 Oct. Legislative Assembly convenes

19 Dec. Louis XVI vetoes decrees against émigrés and unsworn priests

1792

20 April. War declared on Austria

25 April. First use of guillotine

13 June. Prussia declares war on France

20 June. Sansculottes invade royal palace

30 June. *Fédérés* enter Paris singing the *Marseillaise*

10 August. Overthrow of monarchy

2–6 Sept. September massacres

20 Sept. First victory of French forces at Valmy

21 Sept. Convention meets

22 Sept. Republic proclaimed

19 Nov. Fraternity and help offered to all peoples 'seeking to recover their liberty'

3 and 26 Dec. Trial of Louis XVI

**1793**

16 Jan. Louis XVI condemned to death

21 Jan. King executed

1 Feb. War against British and Dutch

11 Mar. Vendée rebellion begins

19 Mar. Defeat in Belgium at Neerwinden

6 April. Committee of Public Safety created

31 May–2 June. Purge of Girondins

June. Spread of 'Federalist Revolt'

13 July. Marat assassinated

27 July. Robespierre joins Committee of Public Safety

23 Aug. *Levée en masse* decree

27 Aug. Toulon surrenders to the British

5 Sept. Sansculottes force Convention to declare terror the order of the day

29 Sept. General maximum on prices

Oct.–Dec. Dechristianization campaign

5 Oct. Revolutionary calendar introduced

9 Oct. Fall of Lyon to Convention's forces

16 Oct. Marie-Antoinette executed

31 Oct. Girondins executed

19 Dec. Fall of Toulon

23 Dec. Vendéans defeated at Savenay

**1794**

4 Feb. Abolition of slavery

24 Mar. Execution of Hébertists

5 Apr. Execution of Dantonists

8 June. Festival of the Supreme Being

10 June. Law of 22 prairial inaugurates 'Great Terror' in Paris

27–8 July (9–10 thermidor). Fall of Robespierre; end of terror

Aug.–Dec. 'Thermidorean Reaction'

18 Sept. Republic renouces all religious affiliations

12 Nov. Jacobin club closed

24 Dec. Invasion of Dutch Republic

1795  1–2 Apr. Germinal uprising of sansculottes

20–23 May. Prairial uprising of sansculottes

8 June. Death of Louis XVII

24 June. Declaration of Verona by Louis XVIII

27 June–21 July. Emigré landing at Quiberon

22 Aug. Constitution of Year III and Two Thirds Law approved

1 Oct. Belgium annexed

5 Oct. Vendémiaire uprising in Paris: 'whiff of grapeshot'

2 Nov. Directory inaugurated

1796  19 Feb. Abolition of *assignats*

11 April. Bonaparte invades Italy

10 May. Arrest of Babeuf and conspirators for equality

1797  18 April. Bonaparte forces peace preliminaries of Leoben on the Austrians

29 June. Cisalpine Republic created

4 September. Councils and Directory purged in coup of fructidor

30 Sept. Bankruptcy of Two Thirds

18 Oct. Peace of Campo Formio ends war on the continent

1798  15 Feb. Roman Republic proclaimed

11 May. Electoral results annulled in coup of floréal

19 May. Bonaparte sails for Egypt

21 May. Irish rebellion

1 Aug. Battle of the Nile. Bonaparte marooned in Egypt

5 Sept. Jourdan law universalizes conscription

1799  26 Jan. Parthenopean Republic proclaimed in Naples

12 Mar. Austria declares war: War of the Second Coalition

THE REVOLUTIONARY CALENDAR: introduced in October 1793 and dating from 22 September, the anniversary of the declaration of the Republic, the calendar remained in official use until 1806. The names of its months, invented by Fabre d'Eglantine, were intended to evoke the seasons, but defy easy translation. Scornful British contemporaries, however, rendered

| Month | Revolutionary year | | | |
|---|---|---|---|---|
| | II | III | IV | V |
| 1 vendémiaire | 22 Sept. 1793 | 22 Sept. 1794 | 23 Sept. 1795 | 22 Sept. 1796 |
| 10 | 1 Oct. 1793 | 1 Oct. 1794 | 2 Oct. 1795 | 1 Oct. 1796 |
| 20 | 11 | 11 | 12 | 11 |
| 1 brumaire | 22 | 22 | 23 | 22 |
| 10 | 31 | 31 | 1 Nov. 1795 | 31 |
| 20 | 10 Nov. 1793 | 10 Nov. 1794 | 11 | 10 Nov. 1796 |
| 1 frimaire | 21 | 21 | 22 | 21 |
| 10 | 30 | 30 | 1 Dec. 1795 | 30 |
| 20 | 10 Dec. 1793 | 10 Dec. 1794 | 11 | 10 Dec. 1796 |
| 1 nivôse | 21 | 21 | 22 | 21 |
| 10 | 30 | 30 | 31 | 30 |
| 20 | 9 Jan. 1794 | 9 Jan. 1795 | 10 Jan. 1796 | 9 Jan. 1797 |
| 1 pluviôse | 20 | 20 | 21 | 20 |
| 10 | 29 | 29 | 30 | 29 |
| 20 | 8 Feb. 1794 | 8 Feb. 1795 | 9 Feb. 1796 | 8 Feb. 1797 |
| 1 ventôse | 19 | 19 | 20 | 19 |
| 10 | 28 | 28 | 29 | 28 |
| 20 | 10 Mar. 1794 | 10 Mar. 1795 | 10 Mar. 1796 | 10 Mar. 1797 |
| 1 germinal | 21 | 21 | 21 | 21 |
| 10 | 30 | 30 | 30 | 30 |
| 20 | 9 Apr. 1794 | 9 Apr. 1795 | 9 Apr. 1796 | 9 Apr. 1797 |
| 1 floréal | 20 | 20 | 20 | 20 |
| 10 | 29 | 29 | 29 | 29 |
| 20 | 9 May 1794 | 9 May 1795 | 9 May 1796 | 9 May 1797 |
| 1 prairial | 20 | 20 | 20 | 20 |
| 10 | 29 | 29 | 29 | 29 |
| 20 | 8 June 1794 | 8 June 1795 | 8 June 1796 | 8 June 1797 |
| 1 messidor | 19 | 19 | 19 | 19 |
| 10 | 28 | 28 | 28 | 28 |
| 20 | 8 July 1794 | 8 July 1795 | 8 July 1796 | 8 July 1797 |
| 1 thermidor | 19 | 19 | 19 | 19 |
| 10 | 28 | 28 | 28 | 28 |
| 20 | 7 Aug. 1794 | 7 Aug. 1795 | 7 Aug. 1796 | 7 Aug. 1797 |
| 1 fructidor | 18 | 18 | 18 | 18 |
| 10 | 27 | 27 | 27 | 27 |
| 20 | 6 Sept. 1794 | 6 Sept. 1795 | 6 Sept. 1796 | 6 Sept. 1797 |
| 1st complementary day | 17 | 17 | 17 | 17 |
| 5th | 21 | 21 | 21 | 21 |
| 6th | | 22 | | |

them: Slippy, Nippy, Drippy; Freezy, Wheezy, Sneezy; Showery, Flowery, Bowery; Heaty, Wheaty, Sweety. Twelve thirty-day months left five days over. These days were originally called *sansculottides*, but under the Directory were relabelled complementary days. Below is a concordance between the revolutionary and Gregorian calendars.

| VI | VII | VIII | IX |
|---|---|---|---|
| 22 Sept. 1797 | 22 Sept. 1798 | 23 Sept. 1799 | 23 Sept. 1800 |
| 1 Oct. 1797 | 1 Oct. 1798 | 2 Oct. 1799 | 2 Oct. 1800 |
| 11 | 11 | 12 | 12 |
| 22 | 22 | 23 | 23 |
| 31 | 31 | 1 Nov. 1799 | 1 Nov. 1800 |
| 10 Nov. 1797 | 10 Nov. 1798 | 11 | 11 |
| 21 | 21 | 22 | 22 |
| 30 | 30 | 1 Dec. 1799 | 1 Dec. 1800 |
| 10 Dec. 1797 | 10 Dec. 1798 | 11 | 11 |
| 21 | 21 | 22 | 22 |
| 30 | 30 | 31 | 31 |
| 9 Jan. 1798 | 9 Jan. 1799 | 10 Jan. 1800 | 10 Jan. 1801 |
| 20 | 20 | 21 | 21 |
| 29 | 29 | 30 | 30 |
| 8 Feb. 1798 | 8 Feb. 1799 | 9 Feb. 1800 | 9 Feb. 1801 |
| 19 | 19 | 20 | 20 |
| 28 | 28 | 1 Mar. 1800 | 1 Mar. 1801 |
| 10 Mar. 1798 | 10 Mar. 1799 | 11 | 11 |
| 21 | 21 | 22 | 22 |
| 30 | 30 | 31 | 31 |
| 9 Apr. 1798 | 9 Apr. 1799 | 10 Apr. 1800 | 10 Apr. 1801 |
| 20 | 20 | 21 | 21 |
| 29 | 29 | 30 | 30 |
| 9 May 1798 | 9 May 1799 | 10 May 1800 | 10 May 1801 |
| 20 | 20 | 21 | 21 |
| 29 | 29 | 30 | 30 |
| 8 June 1798 | 8 June 1799 | 9 June 1800 | 9 June 1801 |
| 19 | 19 | 20 | 20 |
| 28 | 28 | 29 | 29 |
| 8 July 1798 | 8 July 1799 | 9 July 1800 | 9 July 1801 |
| 19 | 19 | 20 | 20 |
| 28 | 28 | 29 | 29 |
| 7 Aug. 1798 | 7 Aug. 1799 | 8 Aug. 1800 | 8 Aug. 1801 |
| 18 | 18 | 19 | 19 |
| 27 | 27 | 28 | 28 |
| 6 Sept. 1798 | 6 Sept. 1799 | 7 Sept. 1800 | 7 Sept. 1801 |
|  |  |  | 18 |
| 17 | 17 | 18 | 22 |
| 21 | 21 | 22 |  |
|  | 22 |  |  |

# Further reading

If this book has achieved its aims, readers will not be surprised to learn
that the literature of the French Revolution is truly vast. Much of the
detailed work is also in French, although there is more of quality in
English than on most historical topics outside the anglophone sphere.
Fortunately most of the books in the following very select list have
substantial bibliographies and often detailed footnotes from which
particular aspects of the subject can be pursued beyond anything
possible in a very short introduction.

## General surveys

M. Broers, *Europe under Napoleon 1799–1815* (London, 1996). Treats the
Napoleonic epic as a prolongation of the Revolution. A *tour de
force*.

W. Doyle, *The Oxford History of the French Revolution* (Oxford, 1989).
Not simply about the Revolution in France, but also its impact on
Europe as a whole.

F. Furet, *Revolutionary France 1770–1870* (Oxford, 1992). The leading
late twentieth-century French authority sets the Revolution in the
longer-term sweep of his country's history.

C. Jones, *The Longman Companion to the French Revolution* (London,
1988). An invaluable compendium of useful information.

A. Mathiez, *The French Revolution* (London, 1928). *The* classic account:
compellingly written with passionate commitment.

S. Schama, *Citizens. A Chronicle of the French Revolution* (London, 1989). The bestseller of the bicentennial year, immensely readable, extremely long, accelerating towards an abrupt conclusion in 1794.

D. M. G. Sutherland, *France 1789–1815. Revolution and Counter-Revolution* (London, 1986). Rich in detail, taking in Napoleon as well as the revolutionary decade.

## Interpretations

T. C. W. Blanning, *The French Revolution, Class War or Culture Clash?* (London, 1998). Spikily readable reflections on the direction of the debate since the 1950s.

A. Cobban, *The Social Interpretation of the French Revolution* (2nd edition, Cambridge, 1999). A reissue of the founding text of revisionism, with an introduction by Gwynne Lewis.

F. Furet, *Interpreting the French Revolution* (Cambridge, 1982). Furet's initial manifesto against the 'Jacobino-Marxist Vulgate'.

G. Lewis, *The French Revolution. Rethinking the Debate* (London, 1993). Vigorously written attempt to salvage classic traditions from a generation of revisionism and post-revisionism.

C. Lucas (ed.), *Rewriting the French Revolution* (Oxford, 1991). Bicentennial lectures by an international panel of authorities.

J. M. Roberts, *The French Revolution* (2nd edition, Oxford, 1999). Thoughtful reflections on the Revolution's ambiguities.

A. de Tocqueville, *The Old Regime and the Revolution* (London, 1988). There are many editions of this most enduring of analyses. This one has a useful introduction by Norman Hampson.

## Origins

R. Chartier, *The Cultural Origins of the French Revolution* (Durham, NC, 1991). Authoritative post-revisionist survey.

W. Doyle, *Origins of the French Revolution* (3rd edition, Oxford, 1999). Contains a historiographical survey as well as an analytical account.

G. Lefebvre, *The Coming of the French Revolution* (Princeton, 1947). The best analysis in the classic tradition.

B. Stone, *The Genesis of the French Revolution. A Global-historical Interpretation* (Cambridge, 1994). Attempts to set the origins in a wider context.

T. Tackett, *Becoming a Revolutionary. The Deputies of the French National Assembly and the Emergence of a Revolutionary Culture (1789–1790)* (Princeton, 1996). Careful analysis of the early stages of the revolutionary process.

**Topics**

F. Aftalion, *The French Revolution. An Economic Interpretation* (Cambridge, 1990).

D. Arasse, *The Guillotine and the Terror* (London, 1989).

N. Aston, *Religion and Revolution in France 1780–1804* (London, 2000). Incorporates thirty years of scholarship since McManners.

T. C. W. Blanning, *The French Revolutionary Wars 1787–1802* (London, 1996).

M. Crook, *Elections in the French Revolution* (Cambridge, 1996).

A. Forrest, *The French Revolution and the Poor* (Oxford, 1981).

H. Gough, *The Newspaper Press in the French Revolution* (London, 1988).

—— *The Terror in the French Revolution* (London, 1998).

P. Jones, *The Peasantry and the French Revolution* (Cambridge, 1988).

D. P. Jordan, *The King's Trial. Louis XVI versus the French Revolution* (Berkeley, 1979).

M. Lyons, *Napoleon Bonaparte and Legacy of the French Revolution* (London, 1994).

J. McManners, *The French Revolution and the Church* (London, 1969). Elegant and moving brief survey, superbly readable.

S. E. Melzer and L. E. Rabine (eds.), *Rebel Daughters. Women and the French Revolution* (New York, 1992).

J. Roberts, *The Counter-Revolution in France 1787–1830* (London, 1991).

G. Rudé, *The Crowd in the French Revolution* (Oxford, 1965).

P. W. Schroeder, *The Transformation of European Politics, 1763–1848*

(Oxford, 1994). The latest thinking on international relations in the age of revolutions.

G. A. Williams, *Artisans and Sansculottes. Popular Movements in France and Britain during the French Revolution* (2nd edition, London, 1988).

## People

I. Germani, *Jean-Paul Marat, Hero and Anti-hero of the French Revolution* (Lampeter, 1992).

N. Hampson, *The Life and Opinions of Maximilien Robespierre* (London, 1974). Brilliant reflections on the problems of interpreting this central figure.

—— *Danton* (London, 1978).

J. Hardman, *Louis XVI* (London and New Haven, 1993). Idiosyncratic biography, at its best before 1789.

C. Haydon and W. Doyle (eds.), *Robespierre* (Cambridge, 1998). Essays on the significance of Robespierre in the Revolution and later.

F. Markham, *Napoleon* (London, 1963). Still the best short introduction to Napoleon's life.

W. Roberts, *Jacques-Louis David, Revolutionary Artist. Art, Politics and the French Revolution* (Chapel Hill, NC, 1989).

R. B. Rose, *Gracchus Babeuf. The First Revolutionary Communist* (London, 1978).

## Legacies

H. Ben Israel, *English Historians of the French Revolution* (Cambridge, 1968). Surveys nineteenth-century debates.

G. Best (ed.), *The Permanent Revolution. The French Revolution and its Legacy, 1789–1989* (London, 1988). Eight distinguished essayists explore the Revolution's enduring importance.

R. Gildea, *The Past in French History* (New Haven and London, 1994). Analyses the haunting of modern French history by revolutionary ghosts.

E. J. Hobsbawm, *Echoes of the Marseillaise. Two Centuries Look Back on the*

*French Revolution* (London, 1990). A Marxist lament for the loss of old certainties.

S. L. Kaplan, *Farewell, Revolution* (2 vols, Ithaca, New York, 1995). Long and wordy, but the fullest account of the bicentenary of 1989 in France. Volume I covers the public commemoration, volume II the historical debate.

J. Klaits and M. H. Haltzel (eds.), *The Global Ramifications of the French Revolution* (Cambridge, 1994). Wide-ranging essays touching some unexpected areas.

# Index

# Expand your collection of
# VERY SHORT INTRODUCTIONS

# HISTORY
## A Very Short Introduction
John H. Arnold

*History: A Very Short Introduction* is a stimulating essay about how we understand the past. The book explores various questions provoked by our understanding of history, and examines how these questions have been answered in the past. Using examples of how historians work, the book shares the sense of excitement at discovering not only the past, but also ourselves.

'A stimulating and provocative introduction to one of collective humanity's most important quests – understanding the past and its relation to the present. A vivid mix of telling examples and clear cut analysis.'

**David Lowenthal, University College London**

'This is an extremely engaging book, lively, enthusiastic and highly readable, which presents some of the fundamental problems of historical writing in a lucid and accessible manner. As an invitation to the study of history it should be difficult to resist.'

**Peter Burke, Emmanuel College, Cambridge**

www.oup.co.uk/vsi/history

# POLITICS
## A Very Short Introduction
Kenneth Minogue

In this provocative but balanced essay, Kenneth Minogue discusses the development of politics from the ancient world to the twentieth century. He prompts us to consider why political systems evolve, how politics offers both power and order in our society, whether democracy is always a good thing, and what future politics may have in the twenty-first century.

'This is a fascinating book which sketches, in a very short space, one view of the nature of politics … the reader is challenged, provoked and stimulated by Minogue's trenchant views.'
**Ian Davies, *Talking Politics***

'a dazzling but unpretentious display of great scholarship and humane reflection'
**Neil O'Sullivan, University of Hull**

www.oup.co.uk/vsi/politics